ARCHITECTURE IN EDUCATION

A Resource of Imaginative Ideas and Tested Activities

Produced by Architecture in Education,
a program of the Foundation for Architecture, Philadelphia.

Edited by   MARCY ABHAU
   with   ROLAINE COPELAND
              GRETA GREENBERGER

Illustrations by   MARCY ABHAU

This publication was made possible
through a generous grant from the
PHOEBE W. HAAS CHARITABLE TRUST

The Foundation for Architecture was created to increase public awareness of Philadelphia's built environment through sponsorship of activities that interpret the city's architectural past, enliven the experience of its architectural present, and influence choices for its architectural future. The Foundation for Architecture promotes the public's active involvement in decisions about the city's buildings, landscapes, parks and urban spaces. As part of its responsibility to the city and to the public, the Foundation encourages the evaluation of issues and opportunities affecting Philadelphia civic design. Programs of the Foundation promote Philadelphia as a Museum of Architecture for all its citizens, and serve as a catalyst for responsible discussion and decision making. Membership is open to all interested individuals and organizations.

Executive Director: John Higgins

Project Directors: Rolaine Copeland
                           Greta Greenberger

Foreward by: Alan Levy

Design, Layout and   Joanne Dhody
Production: Lauren Castle

Special thanks to: Margaret Carlin for her enormous help and
                           encouragement with the original manuscript.

ISBN 0-9622908-0-7

Second printing 1989.

Third printing 1992.

Fourth printing 1996.

DEDICATION

This resource book is dedicated to the memory of Dorothy Haas, as a tribute to her concern for our greatest resource -- the young minds which will shape our future; and to Dr. F. Otto Haas, whose interest in improving the environment in which we live has helped to create, encourage and nurture the education activities of the Foundation for Architecture.

FOREWORD

The quality of our built environment involves more than making it work properly. It also demands a level of design that supports and nourishes the aspirations of our society and our culture. To enrich that environment, protect it, possess it as our own, we must learn more about it. We must understand it as a part of history, of both local history and the more remote past, upon which much of it is based.

Built environmental education can be viewed as a case of learning about the familiar in a fresh new way, understanding how it got to be that way, and discovering how we might change it. Classrooms and schoolyards are rich laboratories immediately accessible for exploration. We must never make the mistake of equating environmental education with the study of "somewhere else". Like so many other lessons, learning about our surroundings begins at home.

Built environmental education is not the private domain of professional architects or city planners either in terms of what should be studied or who should teach it. Although teachers can benefit greatly from the participation of architects and other design students and professionals in the classroom, teachers can be confident in their own knowledge acquired through experience. What makes it so much fun to learn, and to teach, is that it is experiential. It is learned by doing, and this motivates students to get involved and stay involved. It can follow any lead a teacher wishes to take, building upon a teacher's own interests. This also creates motivated teachers.

There are many "environments" to draw upon: the immediate environment of the home, school and neighborhood; the bigger, commercial and institutional environment of downtown. There are the environments of our forefathers, of people living in far away places, of past cultures like the Middle Ages, Ancient Rome and Greece, to explore. There are the environments of Gothic cathedrals, Renaissance palaces, English and Japanese gardens, skyscrapers and many other well known architectural monuments to investigate.

Built environment education can be a special content area or a vehicle for learning about something else -- social studies, science, art, mathematics or history -- in a way that heightens learning. The built environment can be studied through drawing, building models, photography, writing stories, interviewing people, taking a trip; by measuring, counting, observing; by reading about it, hearing someone talk about it; and by getting involved in changing it.

Change is the natural state of the built environment. Learning about our environment helps us direct that change toward better places to live, learn and work. We must understand the forces involved in shaping our environment so that we can participate in its development and play an active role in its future. The survival of our society and our culture depends on it.

– Alan Levy

HISTORY OF THE ARCHITECTURE IN EDUCATION PROGRAM

In 1981 the Foundation for Architecture, in cooperation with the Philadelphia School District, the University of Pennsylvania, Temple University, and local architecture firms, initiated a Program for the Philadelphia public school system which enables students from kindergarten through twelfth grade to learn about architecture and the built environment.

Over one thousand Philadelphia School District students participate in the Program each year. In addition, several hundred more young people from other school districts and independent schools in the Delaware Valley participate in the expanded AIE Program. The Program's unique capability to fit into the existing standardized curriculum in the subject areas of **SOCIAL STUDIES**, **LANGUAGE ARTS**, **SCIENCE**, **MATH** and **FINE ARTS** demonstrates its interdisciplinary quality.

The content of the Program is based on an outline of basic concepts about architecture and the built environment. These concepts reflect three broad areas of study: **perceptual**, **social** and **technological**. This is a comprehensive approach to learning and forms the basis for the interdisciplinary, sequential character of the program.

A professional architect, a university architecture student and usually two teachers work together to provide the appropriate lessons, materials and activities for the class. At the general opening meeting and following planning sessions, staff consultation and curriculum development are the major emphases. Through concept development, sharing of teaching methods, and implementation of activities, teachers gain knowledge and understanding of the built environment which enables them to further develop subject material. In the past five years of the Program the architects have contributed over 1500 volunteer hours each year.

Participating teachers and community organization leaders are involved in curriculum development through the Foundation for Architecture's AIE staff and extensive Resource Center. The Center includes visual materials, case studies, books, worksheets, tested activities, teacher and student workshops, and this curriculum overview: *Architecture in Education: A Resource of Imaginative Ideas and Tested Activities.*

The value of the Architecture in Education Program is evident and its accomplishments are far-reaching, as evidenced by the school students' tremendous enthusiasm. They become aware of the issues which foster a more livable city; they learn to understand the effect environment has on behavior; they see how they can influence potential change for a better environment. These young people are the decision makers, the neighborhood and city leaders of the future.

Rolaine Copeland, Director
Architecture in Education Program
Foundation for Architecture
Philadelphia

ACKNOWLEDGEMENTS

Hermine Mitchell, Past Chair of the Architecture in Education Advisory Committee: for originating the Program and for maintaining her dedication throughout its development.

Leslie M. Gallery, AIA, Founding Director of the Foundation for Architecture, Philadelphia: for inspiring new directions for the Program's growth.

The AIE Advisory Committee: for organizing and implementing the combined ideas of the Program's many contributors, and continuing to advise as the Program expands.

The Board of Trustees of the Foundation for Architecture: for encouraging and advising the Program's development and expansion.

The Architects and Architecture Firms of Philadelphia: for volunteering their time, knowledge and affection. The vitality they bring to the Program has made it outstanding in the country.

The University of Pennsylvania and **Temple University**: for advising the Program through their own Departments of Architecture and for encouraging their architecture students to become valuable members of the teaching teams.

The Philadelphia School District: for affirming the Program's educational value by integrating it into many of its schools' curricula. Special thanks to **Dr. Constance E. Clayton**, Superintendent of Schools; **Dr. Rita Altman**, Associate Superintendent; **Herman Mattleman, Esq.**, President of the School District of Philadelphia Board of Education; **Harry Bonelli**, Director of Division of Art Education, **Dr. George French**, Past Director of Division of Social Studies; **Harold Kessler**, Director of Division of Social Studies; **Marvin Robinson**, Assistant Director, Division of Social Studies; **Thomas Rosica**, Executive Director of Categorial Programs; and the **Principals** and **Teachers** who have implemented the Program in their schools and classrooms.

The Funding Contributors: for their generous support and recognition of the Program's value in shaping the attitudes of our future leaders: **The Barra Foundation, The Hunt Manufacturing Company, The Pennsylvania Humanities Council, The Philadelphia Foundation, The Philadelphia Savings Fund Society**, and the **Phoebe W. Haas Charitable Trust**.

First Printing (1986):

Second Printing (1989):

HOW TO USE THIS BOOK

The activities that follow encompass a variety of perceptual, social, and technological issues as they relate to the built environment. The Table of Contents gives an overview of each chapter which is repeated on the appropriate divider page. Generalizations in the beginning become more specific as vocabulary is developed and planning techniques are explained. The activities are organized to present a coherent, cumulative series, although it is hoped that educators will adapt them to their own curricular agendas.

The activities tend to adapt easily to a wide range of sophistication and skill levels. Approximate **grade levels** are listed at the lower left of each entry. These levels are not restrictive, but are meant as reminders that certain topics may be too abstract for the primary grades, and that some handouts have been prepared in a simplified form that may be inappropriate for upper grades. More sophisticated and detailed information on specific topics is available in books listed in the BIBLIOGRAPHY.

The capital letters below each activity are abbreviations for the subject areas related to that activity: **S** = science, **M** = math, **SS** = social studies, **LA** = language arts, **A** = art. (Cognitive skills involved in visual thinking, such as pattern recognition, scale transformation, and shape discrimination are considered crucial to developing science and math concepts and are so designated.) The related subjects are repeated in the CURRICULUM GUIDE, which can be used as a quick index for lesson planning.

Many of the activities describe extensions or variations on a particular theme. In these cases, the abbreviations and symbols at the end of a paragraph show shifts in grade level or curricular focus within the same activity title.

•   •   •

Realizing that "there is nothing new under the sun," we recognize that many of these activities reflect the efforts and ideas developed nationwide by architects and educators interested in built environment education. Many of their outstanding publications are listed in the BIBLIOGRAPHY.

CURRICULUM GUIDE

TEACHING AIDS

DESIGN

CURRICULUM GUIDE

CURRICULUM GUIDE

CURRICULUM GUIDE

CURRICULUM GUIDE

CURRICULUM GUIDE

TABLE OF CONTENTS

Page

Vocabulary: As topics in built environment education are so varied, there is great potential for vocabulary development in many areas. Vocabulary lists are useful not only for integration into a language arts curriculum but also to serve as a brainstorm-style set of ideas for further study. This section gives ideas for ways to introduce and reinforce new words for students, and includes an illustrated glossary of basic architectural terms. Specific vocabulary lists are placed throughout each section.

Slides: The visual impact of the built environment provides many opportunities for slide presentations developed according to curricular topics. This section offers some suggestions for themes.

These activities focus on general design principles without using any specialized vocabulary. These principles are essential to the nature of architectural planning and should be recalled throughout later projects.

The materials used in the built environment are so important that they merit attention in themselves. Their qualities create an immediate impact on our senses and also determine structural limits and possibilities. Both of these aspects, the sensory and the structural, should be experienced and discussed by students and used as reference points in further study.

Foundation for Architecture, Philadelphia

Page

Page

CITIES

Issues in community and city planning are presented as students begin cumulative and cooperative projects. Taking into account previous lessons, students plan and construct a model community based on various aspects of public and private life.

Focus on Philadelphia: Educators in the Delaware Valley have a great resource in Philadelphia, a city which was carefully planned by William Penn and Thomas Holme in 1682 and is today a virtual "museum of architecture." Much of its original form and structures remain intact, and succeeding generations of technological development and stylistic changes are clearly evident. Many of Philadelphia's architects and much of its architecture are known internationally. The Philadelphia Foundation for Architecture can help develop tours or provide further information for a class trip. These activities are appropriate for students who live in or around Philadelphia, although they can be adapted to other cities.

BIBLIOGRAPHY

Topics in built environment education are so extensive that this publication can only hope to suggest the many possible directions. This Bibliography lists some of the many first-rate books developed for the classroom according to specific topics. Some may be currently out of print, but all are available at the Resource Center of the Foundation for Architecture, Philadelphia.

TEACHING AIDS

Vocabulary: As topics in built environment education are so varied, there is great potential for vocabulary development in many areas. Vocabulary lists are useful not only for integration into a language arts curriculum but also to serve as a brainstorm-style set of ideas for further study. This section gives ideas for ways to introduce and reinforce new words for students, and includes an illustrated glossary of basic architectural terms. Specific vocabulary lists are placed throughout each section.

Slides: The visual impact of the built environment provides many opportunities for slide presentations developed according to curricular topics. This section offers some suggestions for themes.

TEACHING AIDS

1. VOCABULARY AIDS
2. ILLUSTRATED GLOSSARY
3. THE BUILT ENVIRONMENT IN ENGLISH LITERATURE
4. THE BUILT ENVIRONMENT IN FOREIGN LANGUAGE STUDY
5. SLIDES

1. VOCABULARY AIDS

There are many ways to introduce and reinforce the meaning and spelling of the many words associated with the built environment:

- Provide an illustrated glossary of selected elements (see examples following).
- Have students refer frequently to the dictionary and encyclopedia, both of which offer many illustrations of architectural terms. (Many terms encountered in literature are either specialized, old-fashioned, regional, British, or foreign, and often have interesting etymologies, as: crenelated, wainscoting, anti-macassar, porte-cochere, chiffarobe, etc.)
- Show slides that illustrate vocabulary words; students will hold up vocabulary cards at appropriate times.
- Place vocabulary cards around the classroom to label elements, structures, functions, qualities, feelings of the built environment.
- Place vocabulary cards on models (doll houses, student-made models).
- Have students label their own drawings.
- Have students find examples of vocabulary words in magazines for a collage.
- Make a large facade outline on paper. Make simple examples of architectural elements and label. Assign different students to affix the element in the proper place.
- Have students take photographs of the built environment during a neighborhood walk. When the prints are developed, students will mount them on a larger sheet of paper and list all of the vocabulary words that they can find in the picture.
- Use vocabulary words to organize a "scavenger hunt" on a walk through the neighborhood.
- Have students draw pictures of structures so that they can not see each other's work. Each student will "dictate" this picture to a partner, who must understand the vocabulary words to re-create the original. Compare and display.
- Use crossword puzzles, word scrambles, and word searches.
- Have students write poems and essays using vocabulary words in context.

Note: Vocabulary lists are included throughout the sections.

K-12   **SS • LA • A**

2. ILLUSTRATED GLOSSARY

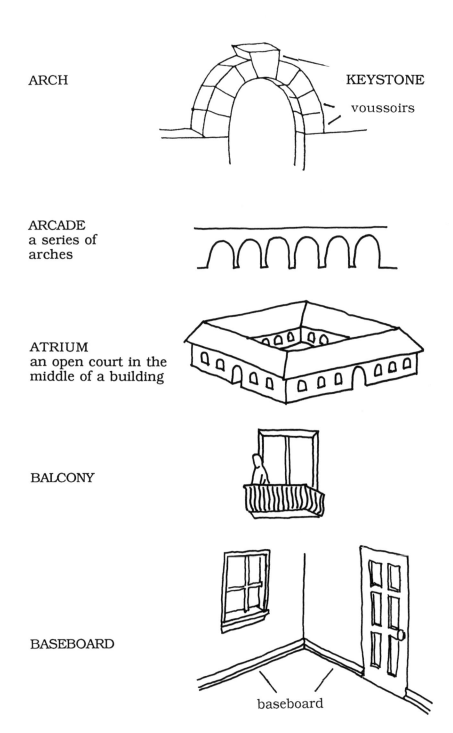

ARCH

KEYSTONE

voussoirs

ARCADE
a series of
arches

ATRIUM
an open court in the
middle of a building

BALCONY

BASEBOARD

baseboard

BUTTRESS

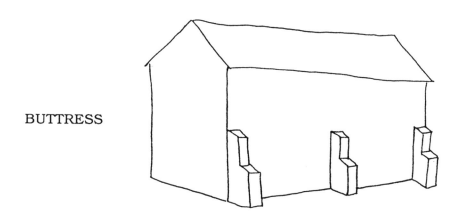

a buttress helps to hold up a wall

FLYING BUTTRESS

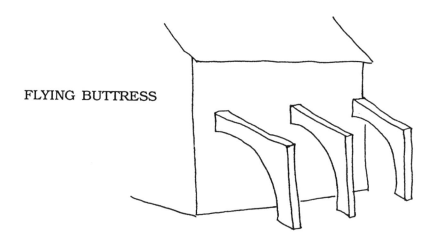

clerestory windows

CLERESTORY

a series of windows
placed high in a wall

Foundation for Architecture, Philadelphia

COLUMN   COLONNADE

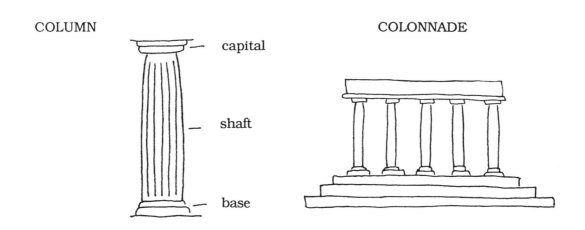

— capital

— shaft

— base

THE THREE ORDERS OF GREEK ARCHITECTURE

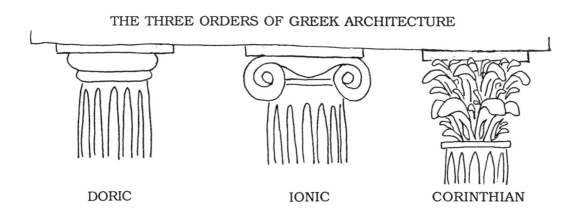

DORIC   IONIC   CORINTHIAN

CORNICE

Foundation for Architecture, Philadelphia

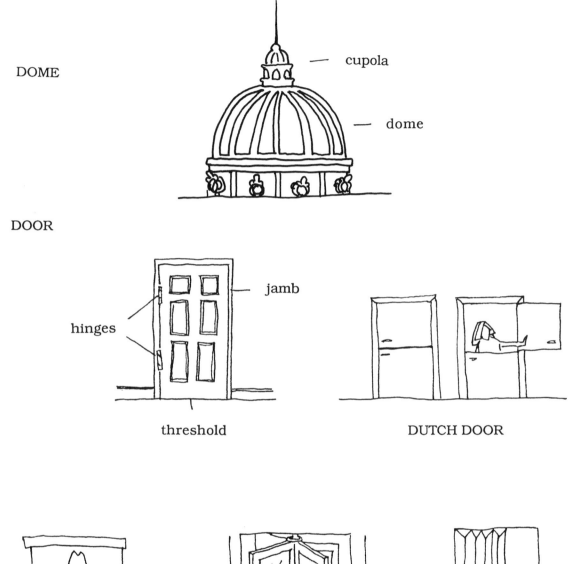

DOME

cupola

dome

DOOR

hinges

jamb

threshold

DUTCH DOOR

SALOON DOOR

REVOLVING DOOR

FOLDING OR
ACCORDION DOOR

DORMERS

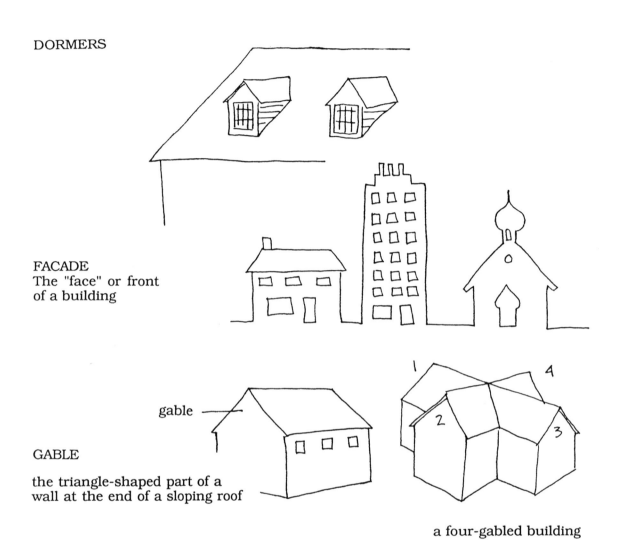

FACADE
The "face" or front
of a building

gable

GABLE

the triangle-shaped part of a
wall at the end of a sloping roof

a four-gabled building

lintels

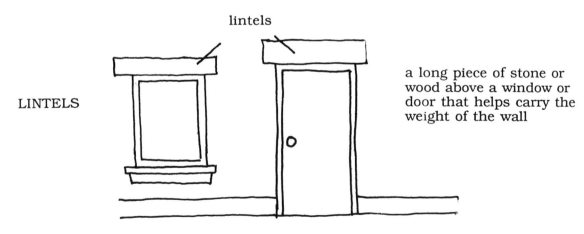

LINTELS

a long piece of stone or
wood above a window or
door that helps carry the
weight of the wall

Foundation for Architecture, Philadelphia

MOLDING

(MOULDING)

strips of curved or carved wood used for decoration

PEDIMENT

a pediment can go over
a door or window

sometimes a pediment has
sculpture in it

a "broken"
pediment

PORCH

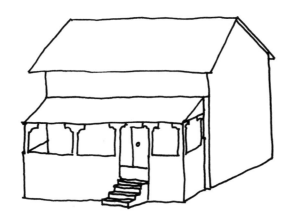

Foundation for Architecture, Philadelphia

QUOINS
large stones used to make
the corner of a building
stronger

ROOFS

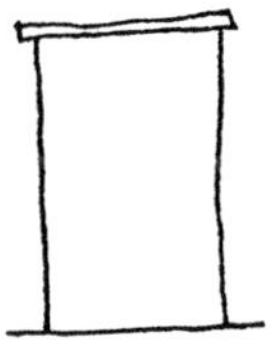

flat 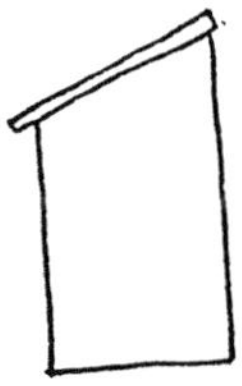   pitched 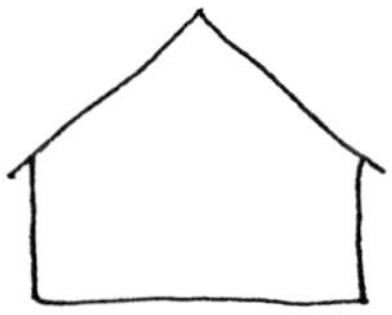   gable

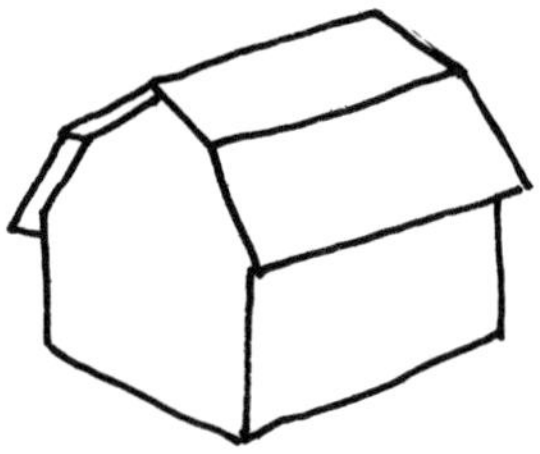

gambrel 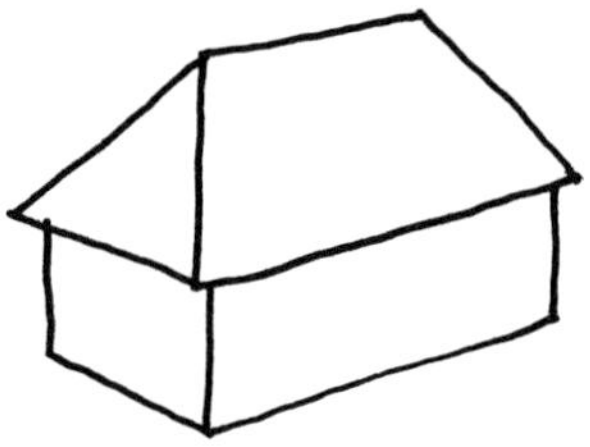   hipped 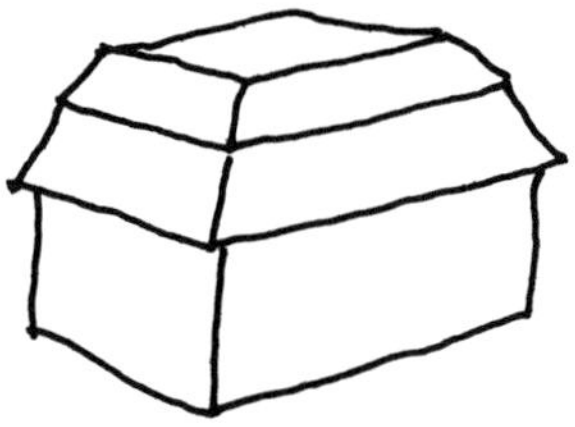   mansard

SKYLIGHT

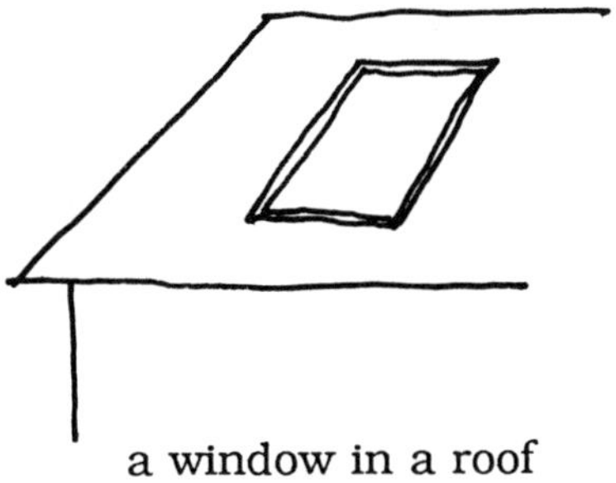

a window in a roof
that lets more light into
a building

STAIRCASE

STAIRWAY

STAIRS

SPIRAL STAIRCASE

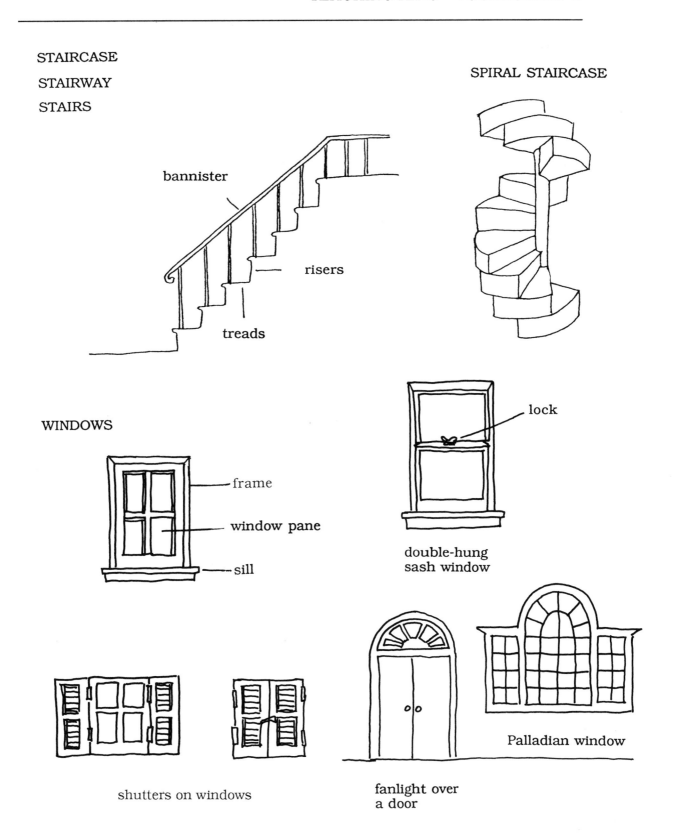

bannister

risers

treads

WINDOWS

frame

window pane

sill

lock

double-hung
sash window

shutters on windows

fanlight over
a door

Palladian window

3. THE BUILT ENVIRONMENT IN ENGLISH LITERATURE

Authors in any language go to great pains to provide readers with vivid descriptions of architectural settings, not only as a backdrop for narrative action but often as an active force in the story. From "The Three Little Pigs" to *The House of the Seven Gables*, literature is full of architectural references. Research shows that *imaging* (developing strong mental pictures) is a crucial aspect of effective reading. Find descriptive passages in basal readers and novels appropriate to your class. When you read aloud to your students, stop periodically and have them discuss what the author wants them to "see" (they might listen with eyes closed). Both in this situation and when students are reading independently, have students draw and color pictures of their images, or develop models of the rooms, buildings, and environments that they read about. Have students apply their writing skills to a description of a familiar environment in which they incorporate vocabulary words, their sensory reactions (color, light, smells, textures, sounds), the emotional qualities of the environment, its dimensions, structure, shape and materials.

K-12

SS • LA • A

Foundation for Architecture, Philadelphia

4. THE BUILT ENVIRONMENT IN FOREIGN LANGUAGE STUDY

Develop a basic architectural vocabulary in a foreign language class. Have students translate the words through illustrations. Students can make pictures or models of architectural landmarks appropriate to the language.

K-12   **SS • LA • A**

Help students determine the ways that architecture expresses the culture behind the language. What qualities are common to the architecture, music, art and crafts of the culture?

K-12   **SS • LA • A**

Find examples of the architecture of the studied language in the United States (Beaux Arts style from France; Greek and Roman styles; Arabic mosques; Spanish-mission style; Italianate style; embellishments of Chinese or Japanese origin).

6-12   **SS • LA • A**

5. SLIDES

Slides are a valuable tool for developing students' sensitivity to both the natural and the built environment. You should have plenty of slides on hand for a particular topic, but be sensitive to the attention span of your students and their capacity to absorb information. Fewer slides with more discussion time will get your ideas across better than too many slides shown to a distracted audience.

There are many ways to develop slide shows:

• **As a Diagnostic and Affective Tool**

All students have an innate sensitivity to architectural qualities. Choose slides that focus on a particular subject and let the **students** provide a spontaneous narration, guided by appropriate questions. This allows students to discover how sensitive they already are to the environment and to begin to organize their impressions and the ideas with an architectural focus. It will also allow you to gauge the level of your students' level of sophistication.

K-12   SS • LA • A

• **To Introduce and Illustrate Vocabulary Words**

Used in conjunction with a visual glossary, slides can illustrate architectural terms which are new to students, as well as show the great variety of design and implementation of these terms and the many variations of each term in actual designs.

K-12   SS • LA • A

• **To Show the Natural Sources for the Built Environment**

Natural environments are comprised of the very structures and materials that ultimately are our resources for design. Taking note of these parallels is an appropriate springboard into a study of the built environment. Tree trunks and animal legs are "columns"; branches "arch" over a street; rocks pile up according to the laws of gravity and weight distribution; a cave provides walls and roof for shelter. We speak of the "skeleton" and "skin" of a house; a facade is a house's "face", with windows for "eyes" and "ears" and a doorway as a "mouth".

K-12   S • SS • LA • A

- **To Show the Natural Environment as a Source for Architectural Materials**

Develop a group of slides that compare a material in its natural setting to the same material after its transformation into a building material. Natural clay becomes a brick, a stone cut from a quarry is incorporated into masonry, trees are converted into beams and furniture, sand is changed into glass, etc. (Implied topics include technology, transportation, economics, ecology, chemistry, and the differentiation between natural and synthetic materials.)

K-12   **S • SS • LA**

- **To Compare the Emotional Impact of the Natural and the Built Environments**

Develop slides of both the natural and the built environments that show a distinct atmosphere. Help your students articulate the moods and emotions of these environments, and elicit what specific elements produce those feelings. (Compare a dark, slippery, scary cave to a dark, mysterious, damp basement; a glade in a high forest to a Gothic cathedral interior; etc.)

K-12   **SS • LA**

- **To Show the Relationship Between the Natural and Built Environments**

Show students images of designs and materials made in harmony with the natural environment as contrasted to buildings constructed at nature's expense. Show slides of gardening and landscaping projects that enhance the built environment.

K-12   **S • SS • LA**

- **To Show How Architecture Has Changed Through History**

History is expressed through architecture. Pyramids, cathedrals, palaces and skyscrapers are graphic indications of technical insights as well as shifts in cultural, political, economic and aesthetic priorities.

K-12   **S • SS • LA • A**

• To Show How Architecture Changes Around the World

Students are fascinated by the variety of human environments. Slides of architectural responses to different climates, land formations, and cultures tie in with a variety of social studies curricula.

As the differences among building types are clearly evident, it is valuable to point out to students (or to ask them to point out) the similarities among them, as an indication of a common bond among disparate cultures.

K-12 **S • SS • LA**

• To Show the Effects of Time on the Built Environment

Buildings and streetways are affected dramatically by climate and human use. Slides can show a building's history as it undergoes wear and tear, disintegration, or redevelopment. Implied issues include the effects of the climate; maintenance and preservation; urban blight and urban renewal; ecology.

Slides of ancient ruins give a very dramatic picture of the long-term effects of weather and neglect.

K-12 **S • SS • LA • A**

• Slides of the School Neighborhood

Show slides of architectural elements in the neighborhood that you can assume are well known to most of the class. For older students, try showing details or shots from an unusual point of view, to see if students can recognize their sources. Let students provide information about the area: How do the local buildings affect them? Which are their favorites? What suggestions might they have for neighborhood improvement? Which parts of the neighborhood do they use most? Which parts have escaped notice? What specific aspects make one building accessible and pleasant, but another one "invisible" or negative?

K-12 **SS • LA • A**

- **Slides of Your City**

Showing slides of well known images in your city will introduce students to the concept of a **landmark**. Students who do not have regular access to the downtown area may be surprisingly unfamiliar with its layout, and may well perceive it mostly in terms of a skyline. Fruitful areas of study include the city's history, historic buildings, the plan behind the street layout, the patterns of public transportation, controversies over the preservation of certain buildings, urban renewal, the benefits and unique qualities of a city park, the arrangement of the neighborhoods, and the dramatic impact of contemporary building projects.

K-12   SS • LA

- **To Facilitate Students' Understanding of Drawing Techniques**

Slides may be projected onto a blackboard or onto white paper; students can then "trace" certain aspects of the slides, leaving a distilled image once the projector is turned off. Examples include: tracing implied perspective lines, tracing the patterns in a facade, discerning the essential proportions of a building.

K-12   S • M • A

- **As a Motivational Tool**

When students are planning a community or a model building, it is useful to show them a number of different slides of various building types at different times throughout their projects (i.e. for five minutes at the start of each work session). Even without lengthy discussion, the images will suggest new ideas, variations and possibilities to the class.

K-12   SS • A

- **To Show the Students and Their Projects**

An effective closure activity is a slide show in which images of students' models are interspersed with images of "real" buildings, as if they were all in the same scale. Students also enjoy seeing slides of themselves at work, and with their finished products.

K-12   SS • A

DESIGN

These activities focus on general design principles without using any specialized vocabulary. These principles are essential to the nature of architectural planning and should be recalled throughout later projects.

DESIGN

6. GEOMETRIC SHAPES: TWO DIMENSIONS

Introduce basic two-dimensional shapes and names:

TRIANGLE   CIRCLE   HALF-CIRCLE   SQUARE   RECTANGLE
SEMI-CIRCLE

Find examples of objects in these shapes around the classroom. With younger students, label the shapes that they find.

Show slides of the built environment and find examples of these shapes.

K-3   **S • M • LA • A**

Project the slides onto the blackboard or onto large paper. Have students trace the geometric shapes and patterns that they find in the picture. Turn off the projector and see the simple design that has been "distilled".

4-12   **S • M • LA • A**

7. GEOMETRIC SHAPES: THREE DIMENSIONS

Show students how three-dimensional shapes can be generated from these two dimensional shapes.

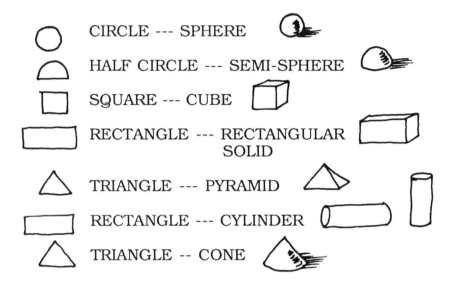

CIRCLE --- SPHERE

HALF CIRCLE --- SEMI-SPHERE

SQUARE --- CUBE

RECTANGLE --- RECTANGULAR SOLID

TRIANGLE --- PYRAMID

RECTANGLE --- CYLINDER

TRIANGLE -- CONE

Let students spend some time drawing these images. Show them how to make "see-through" boxes and pyramids. This activity will help them understand the transition from two to three dimensions.

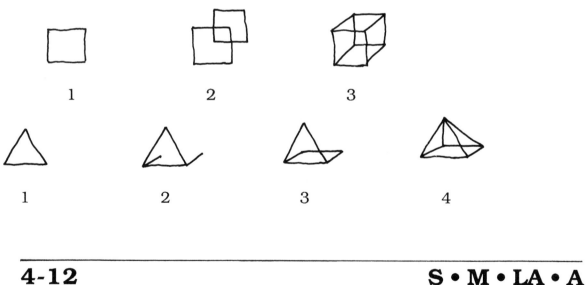

1   2   3

1   2   3   4

S • M • LA • A

Foundation for Architecture, Philadelphia

8. GEOMETRIC SHAPES IN THE BUILT ENVIRONMENT

Show slides of the built environment and have students find examples of both two- and three-dimensional shapes.

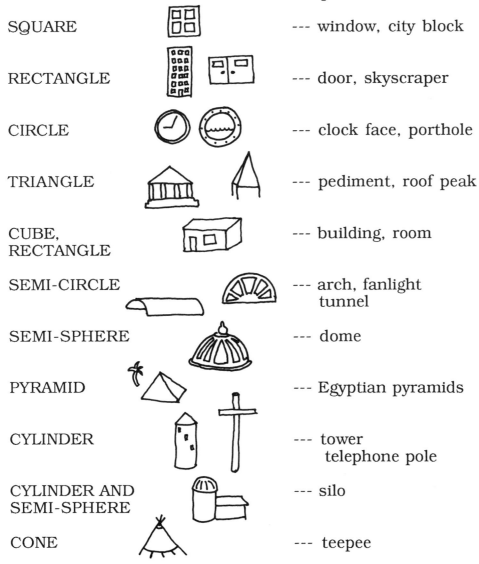

SQUARE --- window, city block

RECTANGLE --- door, skyscraper

CIRCLE --- clock face, porthole

TRIANGLE --- pediment, roof peak

CUBE, RECTANGLE --- building, room

SEMI-CIRCLE --- arch, fanlight tunnel

SEMI-SPHERE --- dome

PYRAMID --- Egyptian pyramids

CYLINDER --- tower telephone pole

CYLINDER AND SEMI-SPHERE --- silo

CONE --- teepee

Using pictures of the built environment from magazines, students find geometric shapes and outline them in thick black marker. These shapes are then traced onto tracing paper to form an abstract pattern, illustrating the names of the shapes.

4-12   **S • M • SS • LA • A**

9. ADDITIVE SHAPES : STREETSCAPES

Prepare simple geometric shapes out of black paper. Give each student a selection of the shapes.

First, the students will simply play with the shapes to make different designs and to become familiar with the shapes. Have the students review the names of the shapes.

Show slides or pictures of the built environment and let the students hold up the appropriate shapes reflected in the slides. After watching the slides, ask students to use their shapes to make a "picture" of a streetscape. Glue into place.

Repeat with shapes cut of various colors, or use white shapes on colored paper; students can add windows, doors, textures and colors.

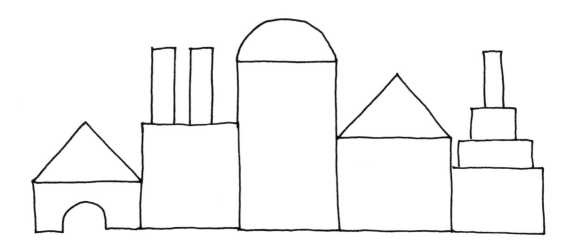

K-4   **S • M • SS • LA • A**

Foundation for Architecture, Philadelphia

10. SYMMETRY AND ASYMMETRY

Use large printed capital letters on pieces of paper folded down the middle to introduce students to the meaning of symmetry and asymmetry. Categorize printed capital letters into symmetric and asymmetric groups.

SYMMETRY

ASYMMETRY

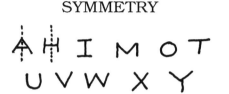

How can you divide B, C, D, E, K to be symmetric?

--B--C--D--E--K---

Demonstrate on pieces of folded paper:

N, S, Z

are in "reverse" symmetry.

--N-- --S--- --Z---

Have students fold pieces of paper in half and make cuts to generate symmetric shapes (as in "doilies" or "snowflakes").

Find examples of symmetry and asymmetry in the classroom and label with the appropriate word.

On a neighborhood walk, find examples of symmetry and asymmetry in building facades. Many facades will provide a mixture of both qualities.

Have students draw examples of symmetric facades and asymmetric facades; or hand out simple cut shapes to be arranged into both kinds of facade designs.

3-12

S • M • LA • A

11. PATTERN COLLAGE

Using old magazines, have students find patterns in pictures of the built environment and glue the images together into a collage. All aspects of the built environment can be included: skyscrapers, windows, roofs and chimneys, man-hole covers, stairways, bannisters, rows of telephone poles, wallpaper designs, etc. Students can use ink markers to emphasize the various patterns that they find. Students can try to think of an adjective to describe each pattern (descriptive or evocative) and add these words to the collage.

K-12   **S • M • SS • LA • A**

12. PATTERN QUILT

Make a copy of the following sheet for each student. Ask them to find shapes that repeat, and explain that repeated shapes make a pattern. Ask students to name the different shapes. Then they may color the shapes in, using a specific color for each shape to reinforce the pattern.

Make a large display by joining all of the students' papers into a large "quilt". Compare with a cloth, knit or crochet quilt that has been made by accumulating many squares.

Show examples of pattern in the built environment through slides or magazine pictures; take a walk through the neighborhood or downtown to see the patterns in doors, windows, roofs, and other architectural elements.

K-4   **S • M • LA • A**

13. A QUILT BLOCK

Foundation for Architecture, Philadelphia

14. HOW DO YOU FEEL ABOUT COLOR?

Hold up sheets of different colors of paper and ask students to name the emotions or feelings that they get from the color. Ask students to explain their associations to the colors.

Ask each student to name a favorite color. They may choose that <u>one</u> color of crayon or colored pencil for this activity. (Have plenty of blue on hand!)

Hand out simple line drawings (p. 24) of familiar objects to the students and tell them to use ONE COLOR ONLY! to fill in each picture. Listen for laughter and groans of disgust as purple horses and pink trees appear. Reflect back to the students the emotions they are expressing as they see the "wrong" colors appear. Remind students of the effect of the green-colored glasses in *The Wizard of Oz*, which gave the illusion of an all-green city.

Hand out two copies of COLOR IN A ROOM (p.26). Have students use color to make one room that they like and another one that they dislike. Compare to see what color elements are common in the "like" rooms and what are common to "dislike" rooms. (Stress the importance of individual taste of a student who "goes against the flow" of popular taste!)

K-12   **SS • LA • A**

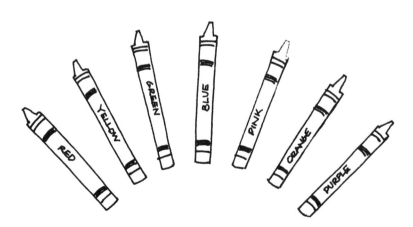

15. ONE COLOR ONLY!

Handout for Activity #14

Foundation for Architecture, Philadelphia

16. "WARM" AND "COOL" COLORS

Introduce the concept of "warm" and "cool" colors. Relate the colors to nature.

WARM	COOL
red - hot coals	blue - water, ice, sky
yellow - sun	green - shady trees
orange - fire	purple - shadows

Show slides of interiors and exteriors that use warm and cool colors to an obvious effect. Ask the students to describe the slides in terms of color use.

Hand out three copies of COLOR IN A ROOM (p.26). Limit students to warm colors for one version and cool colors in the second. Students have free range in the third version. Compare final results and notice how students combine warm and cool colors in the third version. Discuss the feelings generated by different versions.

K-12   **SS • LA • A**

Foundation for Architecture, Philadelphia

17. COLOR IN A ROOM

Handout for Activities #14 and #15.

Foundation for Architecture, Philadelphia

18. TEXTURE RUBBINGS

Collect many small (hand sized) objects with a variety of textures. Suggestions:

rocks	fabric scraps:	coin
nuts	velvet	tennis ball
fruit	canvas	golf ball
vegetables	brocade	rubber ball
feather	cotton ball	soft clay
hairbrush	damp sponge	wet bar of soap
comb	sea shells	tube of toothpaste
bottlecap	cork	rabbit's foot
cold spaghetti	bread	

Have students shut their eyes, wear blindfolds, or hold the objects behind their backs. They will try to think of **adjectives** to describe the textures that they feel. (Guessing what the object is will be a natural impulse, but is not the objective; keep students focussed and insist on at least one adjective per object.) Older students might work in pairs and dictate to a partner. The class will generate a list of all the textural adjectives they can think of; surface temperatures and all other surface qualities should be included **except color**. Possible adjectives include:

hard	sharp	furry	slippery	dry
rough	fuzzy	sticky	moist	smooth
soft	pointed	bouncy	gooey	squishy
stiff (rigid)	crumbly	scratchy	slimy	bendy (flexible)

As the list develops, put the words on separate pieces of paper to make "texture labels". Once students have exhausted their vocabularies and all of the objects have been fully examined, shift the students' attention to the classroom itself, and try to find the same textures in the walls, ceiling, flooring, carpets, windows, desks, doors, shelving, etc. Focus on the built environment (not on the students' clothing or all the junk in their cubbies or lockers), and put the texture labels where they are appropriate.

Discuss with the students the variety of textures that were designed into their environment by the people who built their school. Have them imagine a room with sandpaper on the walls, a floor made of soap, windows made of brick, desks made of rubber and chairs with seats of cold spaghetti. By suggesting inappropriate uses for building materials, students can become more aware of the reasons specific materials were chosen.

Finally, have each student find five different surface textures in the room and make a rubbing of each. Provide strong paper (newsprint will rip) and old crayons to be peeled and used on their sides. Pencils are good for smaller, more intricate rubbings; paper should be taped in place or held firm by a partner. Each rubbing should be labelled as to its quality, the material and the location. Older students can include the reason that material was used.

Students may extend their collection of rubbings in a notebook that includes the rest of the school, home, and exterior materials (manhole covers, brick patterns, masonry, iron work, paved surfaces, etc).

Students may take rubbings of natural surfaces (different tree barks, leaf patterns, rock surfaces) and find similarities between man-made and natural textures.

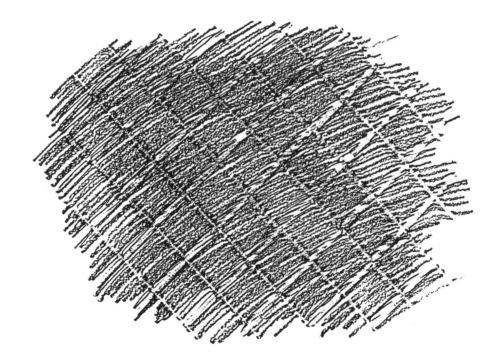

K-12 **S • LA • A**

19. A BLINDFOLD WALK THROUGH SCHOOL

This activity enables students to focus on their non-visual senses. Have students choose partners. One partner will wear a thin blindfold (to let some light in). The other partner will record the blindfolded student's reactions. Go to various areas of the school and let the blindfolded student answer the questions. Swap roles.

What types of materials can you identify by **touch**?
How do the different materials **feel** on your hand - Hot?   Cold?
                                                        Rough? Hard?
Can you find a hard material?   A soft material?
Do you feel cold?   Hot?   Normal?   Does the temperature change?
Where is the **light** coming from? How many different sources and
       types of light can you find? (You can "see" the light even with
       your thin blindfold.)
What noises do you **hear**?   Are they loud?   Do they bother you?
Is there an echo here?
What can you **smell**?   Where do the smells come from?
Would you ever **taste** anything here?
What does the floor/ground **feel** like? How does it sound when you
       walk on it?   With sneakers?   With shoes?
What do people do here?
Does this space make you feel comfortable?   Happy?   Sad? Does
       it make you feel anything at all?

4-12   **S • SS • LA • A**

Students can use this information to write an essay to describe the way certain environments made them feel. They should be specific as to which aspects of the environment contributed to their feelings, giving reference to their senses. Students might try to draw a picture of their non-visual impressions.

4-12   **S • SS • LA • A**

20. CHILD SCALE/ADULT SCALE

Join your class together on the floor. Ask one student to stand up against a large piece of newsprint tacked to the wall. Trace a silhouette of his body. Compare his silhouette to that of an adult's tacked up next to the child's. Measure how many "hands high" the child is, using his hand. Then measure the adult's using his hand. Compare and discuss.

Compare the size of a child's desk and chair to the child, then compare them to an adult. Compare the adult's chair to the child. Ask him if he feels comfortable sitting in the chair. Discuss the relative size and proportion of the furniture to the adult and to the child.

Discuss the relative scale of doors and windows to an adult and then to a child. Stress the idea that a door must be tall enough to walk through, and a window must be high enough to look through. Ask the students how far the window sill comes up to them when they look out of a window. Use this as a reminder when the children are working on an activity and are having difficulty placing windows.

Seat students in groups of five or six at work tables. Hand out printed sheets of paper with the outline of a big and a small house. Explain that the person standing next to each house lives in that house. Pass out the pre-cut windows and doors. Ask the children to place the doors and the windows so that the person can look out. Stress the window sill height. Allow the children to glue the pieces after checking their placement.

Foundation for Architecture, Philadelphia

21. MAKE A PERSON TO FIT EACH BUILDING

Show how BIG or LITTLE a person would be for each of these homes.

Foundation for Architecture, Philadelphia

22. HOW BIG IS A PERIOD?

Give each student a square piece of paper (8" x 8"). Ask that each student make a dot of any size. Ask to have handed back to you an example of a very small dot, a medium sized dot, and the largest in the class. (Have prepared a dot which covers almost the entire paper, in case none of the students makes one that size.) Tape these examples to the blackboard, and ask the students to imagine that these dots are now periods in sentences with different sized letters. Make up a short sentence ("I like pizza.") and show the size of the letters that would fit each period.

The immense dot will require huge letters which you can make on the blackboard. Ask the students if they can think of a place where they have seen such large letters (billboards). Explain that the letters can change **size**, but that they must stay in **scale** with the period.

Show examples from magazines of different sizes of type or shifts of scale from one picture to another.

Foundation for Architecture, Philadelphia

23. HOW BIG IS THIS BUILDING?

Draw on the blackboard a simple picture of two buildings:

Ask students, "How big are these buildings?" Expect some disagreement and confused guesses. Then add to these drawings:

"Now, how big are the buildings?"

Hand out a copy of several simple images of buildings of different sizes and have students draw a figure in scale with each image (see handout on page 31).

Point out the difference between **size** and **scale**. It is useful to ask repeatedly, "Does it **fit**?" ("Could a person fit inside the door?")

You are introducing the concept of **context**, and how an object's context affects its scale.

K-12   **S • M • A**

Foundation for Architecture, Philadelphia

24. DOES EVERYTHING FIT TOGETHER?

Give students two handouts with these two images:

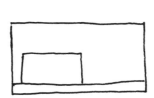 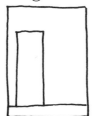

They are to turn each rectangle into a building of any sort they choose. They must add to each picture:

- – at least one door
- – at least one window
- – at least one tree
- – at least one person

When they are finished, compare the drawings in terms of scale. Can each person fit into the door of the building? Could the person look out the windows? Is the size of the tree in a reasonable scale to the building?

Students may need to re-do the exercise with attention to correct scale relationships.

3-8   **S • M • A**

25. SCALE DETERMINANT: PIPE CLEANER PERSON

Give each student one pipe cleaner to be cut and twisted to resemble a human figure. Students should measure their figures and estimate how tall a house would be to fit the figure's scale; then make a drawing of the house, adjusting it as necessary to be sure that the figure "fits" (doorway, steps, windows, family members, pets, etc.) This figure can be kept and used as a scale determinant for further drawings and constructions.

K-12   **S • M • A**

Foundation for Architecture, Philadelphia

26. AN INTRODUCTION TO ONE-POINT PERSPECTIVE

The concept of perspective is highly synthetic and extremely abstract. The system of one-point perspective may be introduced in the younger grades, but students should not be expected to "get it" completely. (Consider that it was not "invented" until the 14th century, although artists had been groping for such a system for years.)

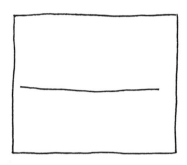

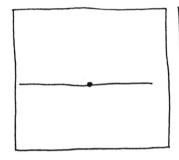

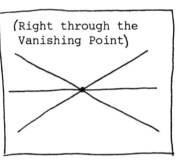

(1) Horizon line (where the sky "meets" the earth)

(2) Vanishing point (shows the direction you are looking)

(3) Construction lines (the tops and bottoms of a row of buildings)

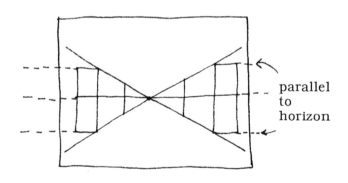

parallel to horizon

(4) sides of buildings

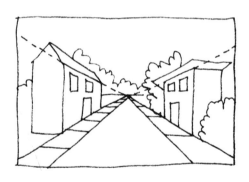

(5) erase construction lines, add facade details - all receding lines must "vanish" at the same point

Foundation for Architecture, Philadelphia

27. PERSPECTIVE ON PLEXIGLAS

Older students can take advantage of a technique used by Renaissance painters to establish perspective lines. Have students work with partners. One partner holds a rectangle of clear Plexiglas (10" x 12" or larger) in place to act as a "window"; the other student simply looks into the Plexiglas and traces the important lines of the image with a grease pencil. Both students must remain still for this exercise to avoid shifts in the image. A long corridor is the best location as there is one specific vanishing point.

Foundation for Architecture, Philadelphia

28. ONE-POINT PERSPECTIVE: WALK TO A VANISHING POINT

Look for a boulevard or street in your area with a wide enough median that students can safely walk along it. Pick a prominent building or other landmark directly **centered** at one end; this will represent the vanishing point. From the most extreme distance, have students make note of the way that the sides of the street appear to **converge** (go together) as they approach the vanishing point. Be sure to make explicit that this convergence is only an **optical illusion**; students know that the lines do not really meet, but it looks as if they do. Artists therefore draw the lines that way to give the impression of deep space. Have students draw or photograph this view; be sure that each student is centrally placed so that the lines will converge at equal angles. Approach the vanishing point in stages; stop at regular intervals and re-draw or re-photograph. Students will notice that the lines still converge at the same angle, but the vanishing point looms larger and larger, until it fills the entire visual field. Sophisticated students will understand that the converging lines continue (in the imagination) beyond the vanishing point to infinity. (The "vanishing point" is an abstract representation of where the lines meet; in this activity you are getting "infinity" to stand still.   These abstractions of reality for the sake of graphic representation are extremely complicated and should elicit quite a discussion!)

4-12   **S • M • LA • A**

Foundation for Architecture, Philadelphia

29. VOCABULARY : DESIGN

asymmetry
collage
color
context
cool colors
design
fit
five senses
   - sight (vision)
   - hearing
   - smell
   - taste
   - touch
geometry
   - triangle, pyramid, cone
   - square, cube
   - rectangle, rectangular solid, cylinder
   - circle, sphere
   - half-circle, semi-sphere

line
measurement
pattern
proportion
relationship
relative size
rhythm
rubbing
scale
scale determinant
shape
size
space
symmetry
texture
three dimensional
two dimensional
warm colors

30. VOCABULARY: PERSPECTIVE

converge, convergence
horizon line
infinity
optical illusion
parallel
perspective, one-point perspective
point of view
vanishing point

K-12   **S • M • SS • LA • A**

Foundation for Architecture, Philadelphia

MATERIALS

The materials used in the built environment are so important that they merit attention in themselves. Their qualities create an immediate impact on our senses and also determine structural limits and possibilities. Both of these aspects, the sensory and the structural, should be experienced and discussed by students and used as reference points in further study.

MATERIALS

31. INVESTIGATING MATERIALS

A look through *Beginning Experiences in Architecture*, by George F. Trogler, is enough to prove that ANY material that can be stacked, bent, cut, twisted, or glued is appropriate for students' investigations. This "exercise" is simply a matter of providing materials and tools and encouraging students to "play" with them. Discussion should follow, during which students can describe the limits of the materials as well as their advantages. For example, a popsicle stick won't bend, but many of them can be stacked up; pipe cleaners are weak in compression (they bend) but are strong in tension and make good joints.

K-12   S • LA • A

32. USEFUL MATERIALS

Following is a list of easily available materials which are valuable for the study of their inherent properties as well as for building model projects.

- **paper** of various weights can be bent, scored and folded to change its structural properties (see STRUCTURES).

- **graph paper** of different sized grids (scale transformations; precision in drawing rectangular shapes, as for floor plans).

- **brown craft paper** in rolls for backdrop murals, street grids.

- **sandpaper** simulates stucco or adobe when glued onto the walls of a model, or can be used as a ground cover for a desert environment; sand poured into paint gives a similar effect.

- **hair curlers** give the effect of an industrial landscape, as do a variety of miscellaneous objects (bottle caps, plastic packing materials, styrofoam forms, spools, bobbins, etc).

- **tin foil** has enough rigidity to stand alone if supported, bent, or twisted, and can be used to suggest aluminum sheeting, stainless steel, mirrors, etc.

- **corrugated cardboard** as an all-purpose building material. Large cartons can become rooms or buildings, or decorated and worn as costumes of architecture; strong standing structures can be made by "slotting".

The corrugation inside the cardboard demonstrates the structural power of the arch; have students pull a piece apart to see that it is nothing but three layers of paper, the middle layer being a series of arches which lend strength.

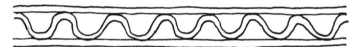

(Corrugated cardboard should be cut with exacto knives under close supervision. Have students score the cardboard first and make a deeper cut afterwards; cuts from the other side may be necessary.)

- **foam board** is a more expensive material, but worth the price for lightweight models.

- **cellophane** in many colors for stained glass windows or to illustrate color mixing.

- **plastic wrap** can cover a domed structure to turn it into a terrarium.

- **pipe cleaners** can be used for various joints or lashings, or to bend into scale figures and furniture.

- **acetate** used with special markers, to compare the inside and outside of a structure.

- **newspaper** for papier mache or to be rolled into newspaper logs, jointed with masking tape, for large trusses.

- **plaster gauze** fuses and strengthens weaker materials.

- **spools** (wood or styrofoam) can be stacked as columns, used as wheels, or used for model-sized furniture.

- **cloth or canvas** for teepees, tents, or temporary walls (hung from clotheslines).

- **sheets** hung up in the room create new environments in the classroom.

- **cardboard tubes** from toilet paper or paper towel rolls can be used to demonstrate the structural strength of the column and used in model constructions; easily decorated.

- **clay** can harden or be dried into facades or models; strengthen with popsicle sticks as a parallel to reinforced concrete; make small bricks.

- **dough** of flour, salt and water can be used as clay, or to revive the art of gingerbread houses.

- **styrofoam** can be used to demonstrate insulation; packing pieces or cups can be cut into decorative elements.

- **shoeboxes** can be used for shoebox diaries and then used to show a structural cut-away or turned into a model building or interior; they can be stacked into modular constructions, as a pueblo or hi-rise city (boxes of all shapes are useful).

- **egg cartons** illustrate the structural strength of the dome and can be used as such in models. Cardboard egg cartons covering walls or ceiling will absorb noise for a lesson in acoustics.

- **sugar cubes** can be stacked into a pyramid.

- **florist foam** is available in large pieces which are easily sawed or cut to make the wedge-shaped voussoirs and keystone in an arch.

- **toothpicks and small marshmallows** are a wonderful combination to let students investigate the structural properties of a truss.

- **plastic straws** can also be used for a truss framework, using bent pipe cleaner pieces as joints; straws can be lengthened by folding (lengthwise) and inserting the end of one into another; scotch tape can repair.

- **sticks** lashed with thread or string make structures used in "primitive" buildings; a frame can be covered with leaves, mud or clay.

- **popsicle sticks** or **tongue depressors** make sturdy frames.

- **children's blocks** are usually cut into shapes with strong architectural reference and often used that way in spontaneous play.

- **waxed cartons** can be cut and inserted into each other to make strong modular units for building projects or can be used singly as building units, as in rowhouses or skyscrapers. Cover with paper to decorate, as the waxy surface repels paint.

- **corks** are easily joined together to parallel the actual sectional construction of stone columns; they can be stacked and decorated as totem poles; they can be sliced and used as floor or wall material in models; cork's qualities (extremely light, absorbs shock and sound, attractive) make it a useful building material, and students will be interested to learn about its source in the bark of trees.

- **cotton** makes wonderful chimney smoke or clouds; cotton can be dirtied to indicate the effects of pollution.

- **string** and **wire** have innumerable uses, not only as structural supports but connected to dowels as power or telephone lines in a model community.

- **string** can also be turned into a tape measure by attaching pieces of tape at one foot intervals. Have students wind their tape measures around a spool (i.e. a toilet paper tube) to prevent hopeless tangles.

- **clotheslines** and **sheets** can be strung throughout a classroom to make new environments or tent structures. Sheets make temporary walls and make dramatic changes in the light, traffic, acoustics, and atmosphere of a room.

- **sponges** cut into different sizes make effective trees and shrubbery for landscaping.

K-12   **S • M • LA • A**

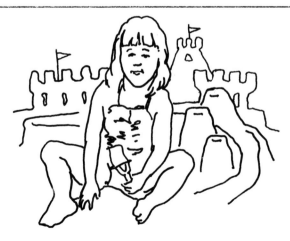

Foundation for Architecture, Philadelphia

33. GRAB BAG OF ARCHITECTURAL MATERIALS

Put examples of different architectural materials inside a bag.
Suggestions:

sticks	carpet	linoleum	plastic
leaves	wood	cork	plaster chip
mud	ceiling tile	rubber	polished marble
stone	cloth	porcelain	different metals
brick	glass	enamel	shingle

In turns, students reach in and choose one object. Before taking it out
of the bag, the students should describe what they feel: texture,
weight, size, etc. Students may guess what the material is; they will
need help in identifying many of the items.

Once all of the items are out of the bag and they are identified, have
the students try to find those materials in context throughout the
classroom, school, outside or at home. Have students draw the
materials **in context**.

Discuss:

- Why are certain materials used in certain places?
  (Strong, easy to clean, lets light in, absorbs sound, flexible,
  etc.)

- What would be a clearly inappropriate material to use for a
  certain purpose? Why? (Why wouldn't you use cork for a
  window or rubber for a floor?)

- Which materials are organic (natural)? Which materials are
  synthetic (man-made)?

K-12   **S • M • LA**

Foundation for Architecture, Philadelphia

34. QUALITIES AND THEIR OPPOSITES

Students can make a chart for each material that is based on opposites, with a center column for mid-way qualities. For example:

MATERIAL: FROSTED GLASS

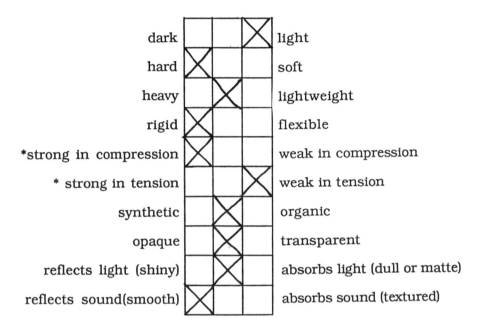

dark			light
hard			soft
heavy			lightweight
rigid			flexible
*strong in compression			weak in compression
* strong in tension			weak in tension
synthetic			organic
opaque			transparent
reflects light (shiny)			absorbs light (dull or matte)
reflects sound (smooth)			absorbs sound (textured)

(The mid-way point between **opaque** and **transparent** is **translucent**, which means that some, but not all, light passes through.)

(* See STRUCTURES.)

4-12   **S • LA**

Foundation for Architecture, Philadelphia

35. COMPARING MATERIALS

Have students develop a matrix that compares the relative qualities of materials:

QUALITIES:

MATERIALS:

	rough	smooth	shiny	soft	hard	rigid	flexible	opaque	translucent	transparent	heavy	lightweight
glass		•	•		•	•				•	•	
stone	•				•	•		•			•	
steel		•	•		•	•		•			•	
clay tile		•	•		•			•			•	
rubber		•		•			•	•				•
wood	•				•	•		•				•

Students will see that some qualities are more readily obtained than others.

Make a word game: List 3 qualities at random and see if students can think of a material that provides them. This activity will be useful for students when they are making choices for their own designs.

4-12   **S • LA**

36. MATERIALS INSIDE THE SCHOOL

Take a walk through school. Take a good look and touch, whenever possible, the materials you find. Choose one room with a specific use (cafeteria, library, utilities room, bathroom) and answer these questions.

1. What materials do you see on the floor?

    Describe the texture of the floor.

    Why is the floor that texture?

    Why is the floor made of that material?

2. What are the walls made of?

    Describe their texture.

    Why were these materials chosen for the walls?

3. What materials are on the ceiling?

    Why were these materials chosen?

    What is the texture of the ceiling?

    Is this a "noisy" or a "quiet" room?

4. What other special materials or textures do you see?

    Where are they used?

    Why do you think they are used?

5. Include at least four rubbings on additional sheets of paper. Write the name of the material, one adjective that describes its texture, and where you found it.

4-12   **S • SS • LA • A**

37. SHOEBOX DIARIES OF MATERIALS

Ask the students to bring in a shoebox from home. This will be a Shoebox Diary. Students will keep a record of the various environments they have been in over a week's time by putting a representative building material from each place into the box. It may be a tile, a shingle, a piece of brick, etc. which in some way gives a description of the particular place. Students will make a record of where they got each item by gluing the item onto a card with the following information:

This is: _____

Where I found it: _____

_____

Date: _____

Once the allotted time is up (each student should have at least ten examples), students will choose one and draw a picture of the place it was found, then glue the item onto the picture to show it in context.

Students who walk to school can make diaries that describe their routes.

3-12   **S • SS • LA • A**

Older students can be directed to find samples of specific materials for their shoeboxes, as in a scavenger hunt.

6-12   **S • SS • LA • A**

38. HOW DO MATERIALS CHANGE OVER TIME?

Show slides of the built environment that focus on the way materials change over time. Suggestions: worn stairs, peeling paint, a billboard being changed, oxidized metal, potholes. Emphasize that some changes come from the effects of the climate (sun, wind, water) and some from human use (wear, re-design). Slides of ancient ruins show these effects dramatically.

Discuss the different ways that different materials show the passing of time (paint blisters, iron rusts, cloth softens and fades in color).

K-12   S • SS • LA

On a neighborhood walk, students will find examples of worn materials. Using a chart, they will make note of the qualities of the materials past and present.

Name of Material	Original Qualities	Where Found	How has it Changed?	Why has it Changed?	Should it be Replaced?
1. bricks	hard, rectangular	sidewalk	cracks, broken parts	weather, people walking on it	some parts
2. marble steps	hard, white	front door	worn down in center	people walking on them	eventually
3. bronze	shiny and bright, gold color, strong	statue	dark and streaky (patina)	weather (air and water)	it could be shined up or painted

4-12   S • SS • LA

Foundation for Architecture, Philadelphia

39. HOW AND WHY DO MATERIALS CHANGE IN DIFFERENT CLIMATES?

Show slides of the built environment from different climates. In class discussion, two main points should be stressed:

1. Different climates provide specific materials because of geologic factors.
   - Arctic: snow and ice (igloo)
   - rain forest: vines, leaves, trees
   - desert: adobe, clay (bricks)
   - deciduous forests: lumber

2. Different materials determine different shapes and structures for human comfort.
   - the ice in an igloo provides insulation from the cold and shelter from wind
   - thick clay walls provide insulation from heat
   - walls of woven leaves and fibers provide ventilation.

K-12   S • SS • LA • A

40. HOW AND WHY DO MATERIALS CHANGE THROUGH HISTORY?

Show slides of historical architectural landmarks. In class discussion, three points should be stressed:

1. the effects of CLIMATE to determine materials

2. the effects of CULTURE (The nature of a structure determines the permanence of its materials, as in the utilization of stone, cliff and earth forms for religious centers as opposed to lightweight poles and fabrics for the homes of nomadic societies.)

3. the effects of TECHNOLOGY (Ancient structures reflect the dependence of builders on human and animal labor, basic tools, and natural forms and materials. As technology developed, materials could be transported more widely and combined into new synthetics, which afforded new possibilities of form that often seem to defy the laws of natural physics. Please refer to the bibliography for more sources on this enormous topic.)

3-12   S • SS • LA • A

41. INSULATION

Discuss with students meaning of insulation and its importance in the built environment. To compare the relative insulating qualities of different materials, have each student bring a shoebox to class. Provide a variety of materials; they will select **one** only to line, cover or enclose the box. Put an ice cube of equal size in each box and put the boxes in an area of even temperature. Use a "control" box that is unlined and another one that is unlined and unlidded; when the ice cube in the unlidded box has completely melted, have students open their boxes and make a quick drawing of how much of the cube is left; the drawings can be displayed in order of "most melted" to "least melted" and should be labelled with the materials used. This experiment can be reversed by heating thermometers in very warm water to an equal temperature, placing them in the insulated boxes, placing the boxes in a cool area, and recording the temperatures after five minutes.

SUGGESTED MATERIALS

pieces of styrofoam	newspaper
tin foil	wet newspaper
wooden tongue depressers	fabric
wax paper	bricks
plastic wrap	sand or dirt
trash bags	clay
cork board	leaves
sponges, wet and dry	foam rubber
blankets	"bubble" packing material
a down vest or jacket	2 foam or feather pillows

Discuss with students the reasons why insulation is sometimes used to keep heat **out** (food storage, hot weather) and sometimes to keep heat **in** (cooking utensils, take-out coffee, clothing, blankets, cold weather).

Show slides of dwellings from different climates to show how building materials and structures are adjusted to hot weather (verandahs, large windows, thick stone walls, light-reflective colors, high roofs, stilts, open-weave walls, fans, air conditioners) or cold weather (thick walls, small windows, insulation, low ceilings, heating systems, solar orientation of windows, trees planted as windbreaks).

Foundation for Architecture, Philadelphia

42. IDEAS FOR RESEARCH PROJECTS ON MATERIALS

Students with independent reading and writing skills can develop their research skills by writing papers about various aspects of materials in the built environment. Potential topics include:

- the transformation of a material from its natural source and form into a building material (clay into brick and tiles, silicone into glass, stone into masonry, elements into alloys, trees into lumber)

- conservation of natural materials used in the built environment

- the history of the technological development of a material (ancient brickmakers, history of glass)

- cumulative lists of a particular material in a variety of contexts and put to different uses, developed over time to allow a student to find it in a variety of environments (as in Shoebox Diaries, but on a more sophisticated level)

- the development of insulation, from primitive materials and systems to modern developments

- the source, qualities, and dangers of asbestos as an insulating material

4-12   **S • SS • LA • A**

43. VOCABULARY: MATERIALS IN THE BUILT ENVIRONMENT

aluminum siding
adobe
alloy
asbestos
asphalt

brick
brick veneer
brick imitation

carpet
ceiling tile
cement
ceramic tile
cinderblock
clapboard
clay
cloth
concrete, concrete block
cork

element

flagstone
flashing
fluorescent
formica

glass
- thermal
- safety
- frosted
- etched
- stained
- mirrored

insulation

leaves
linoleum
lumber

material
marble
masonite
masonry
metal
- iron, cast iron, wrought iron
- lead
- copper
- brass
- tin
- aluminum
- steel, stainless steel
- rust
- patina
mortar

neon

paint
parquet
plaster
plastic
pole

shingle
slate
spackle
sticks
stone
stucco

tar
tar paper
terra cotta
tile

vinyl
veneer

wallboard
wall paper
wood varieties
wood inlay
wood panelling
wood veneer

Foundation for Architecture, Philadelphia

44. VOCABULARY: QUALITIES OF MATERIALS

brittle
crush-proof
flexible ("bendy")
fragile
hard
high insulation
light absorptive (dull)
light reflective (shiny)
low insulation
non-porous
opaque
organic
porous
rigid (stiff)
sound absorptive (textured)
sound reflective (smooth)
strong (in tension, in compression)*
synthetic (man-made)
translucent (cloudy)
transparent (clear)
water repellent
weak (in tension, in compression)*

textures:
- rough
- smooth
- bumpy
- slimy
- crumbly
- sharp
- hard
- soft
- slippery
- clammy
- scratchy
- fuzzy
- furry
- furrowed
- soggy
- liquid
- solid
- springy
- bouncy
- sticky
- dull
- gooey
- squishy
- dry
- moist
- hairy

* See STRUCTURES

K-12

S • LA • SS

STRUCTURES

These simple exercises give insight into essential principles of building construction. Many can be developed to demonstrate some of the basic laws of physics.

STRUCTURES

45. STRUCTURES IN NATURE

Show slides or use picture books to elicit discussion with students about ways in which the natural world provides the basis for human structures in terms of form, materials and construction principles.

NATURAL or ANIMAL STRUCTURE	HUMAN COUNTERPART
pile of stones; hill	pyramid, ziggurat, dome
cave, cocoon	room
tree trunk	column, pillar, post
tree branch	beam, cantilever
spider web	triangulation, truss, cable, suspension bridge
beaver lodge	mortared wall, dome
beaver dam	dam
den, burrow, lair	insulated "rooms" protected from weather
bird, squirrel and chimpanzee nest	tree house
turtle shell, egg shell	portable home, trailer, tent
turtle shell, porcupine quills	armor, fort
underground tunnels and hills of ants, termites and prairie dogs	subway system, tunnel, corridor
honeycomb	modular building based on repeated form
beehive	dome

K-12

S • SS • LA

Foundation for Architecture, Philadelphia

46. BUILDINGS COMPARED TO HUMAN ANATOMY

It is entirely appropriate to compare aspects of a building to human anatomy:

- facade: face (the words are, in fact, related etymologically)
- door: mouth
- windows: eyes and ears
- outside walls: skin
- structural framework: skeleton
  (architects commonly use the terms "skin" and "skeleton" in these ways)
- electrical system: nervous system
- plumbing system: digestive & excretory systems
- ventilation: respiration (a building must be able to "breathe")

K-12   **S • LA**

Students get the most insight into basic building principles by acting them out. The following pages can be used for hand-outs as suggestions for ways that students can feel physical pressures on their own bodies. The arrows indicate the direction of force. A basic vocabulary is included for grades 4-12, though the demonstrations are cogent for younger students as well.

K-12   **S • LA**

Foundation for Architecture, Philadelphia

47. BASIC VOCABULARY OF STRUCTURAL PRINCIPLES

gravity: the pull of the earth that makes objects feel heavy; most easily felt as a downward force

weight: heaviness; the "pull" downwards of gravity

support: to hold something up; in post and lintel construction, the posts are the support

load: weight; in post and beam construction, the weight of the wall above the lintel is the load

span: (noun) the distance between; (verb) to cross the distance between two objects

thrust: a strong push in a certain direction

stress: the way a material reacts to weight; the two forms of stress are tension and compression

tension: stretching; pulling apart

compression: smashing; pushing together (find the word <u>press</u> in compression)

Draw a horizontal line along the edge of a sponge and divide it into equal sections. When you bend the sponge, one side will always be S T R E T C H E D; the divisions will get spread larger. This part of the sponge is <u>in tension</u>. The other side of the sponge will be SMASHEDTOGETHER; the divisions will get smaller. This part of the sponge is <u>in compression</u>.

 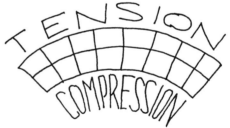

Some materials are strong in tension, as a steel cable. Some materials are strong in compression, as a brick. Architects must choose different materials according to whether the weight is pushing or pulling that part of the structure.

4-12   **S • LA**

Foundation for Architecture, Philadelphia

48. ACTING OUT STRUCTURES

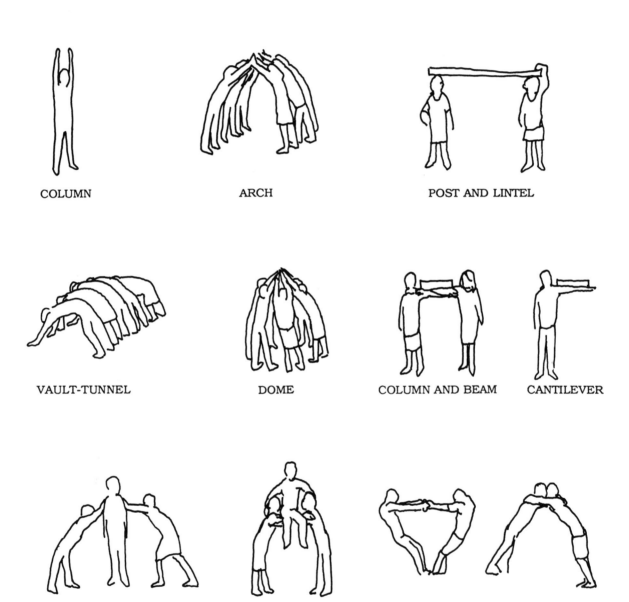

COLUMN   ARCH   POST AND LINTEL

VAULT-TUNNEL   DOME   COLUMN AND BEAM   CANTILEVER

FLYING BUTTRESSES   LOAD AND SUPPORT   TENSION   COMPRESSION

Foundation for Architecture, Philadelphia

49. THE COLUMN

A column is a vertical (upright) support member. We often think of columns as being round, but even a steel girder used as an upright support is considered a column.

Use toilet paper or paper towel tubes to demonstrate that a paper column is weak in one direction (lying on its side), as it can be crushed by a heavy book, but it is very strong when standing up and can support the same book. Arrange four tubes of equal size into a square a few inches apart. Ask students to guess how many books the columns will support. Get a guess from each student, and have them carefully pile books up. Once the tubes are crushed, or the pile gets too high or too unstable to be safe, make estimates of the amount of weight the books represent. Weigh accurately and compare to the weight of the tubes.

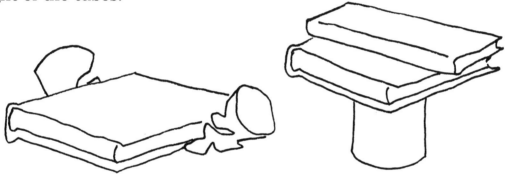

Use slides to introduce the three orders of Greek columns (Doric, Ionic, Corinthian). Find examples from well known local landmarks and from the neighborhood.

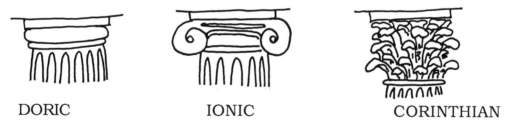

DORIC   IONIC   CORINTHIAN

Give each student one cardboard tube and provide a variety of materials for students to applique and decorate them. Students may use more columns to construct a building which integrates these columns in terms of structure and design.

K-12   **S • SS • LA • A**

50. THE BEAM

A beam is a horizontal structural member supported by one, two or more columns. It is part of the skeleton of a building, and is easily illustrated using a ruler or yardstick supported with blocks or books.

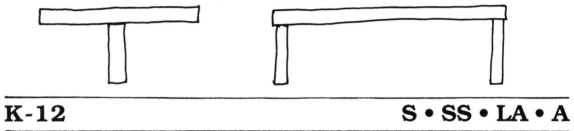

K-12   **S • SS • LA • A**

51. THE CANTILEVER

A cantilever is a beam that is only supported at one end.

Illustrate the word cantilever with piles of books or bricks:

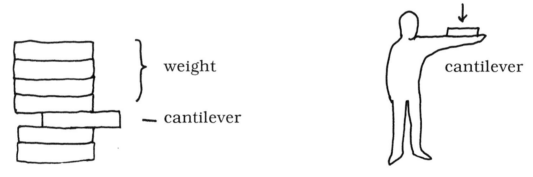

Find examples of cantilever constructions in stairways and balconies.

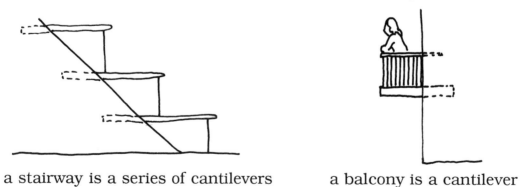

a stairway is a series of cantilevers   a balcony is a cantilever

K-12   **S • SS • LA • A**

Foundation for Architecture, Philadelphia

52. THE POST AND LINTEL

Some of the earliest builders used the post-and-lintel principle of construction to span openings in a wall (doors and windows). Before the invention of the arch, they used two vertical beams (posts) to support the horizontal beam (lintel). The Egyptians used papyrus plants bundled together for posts. The lintel was often a palm log.

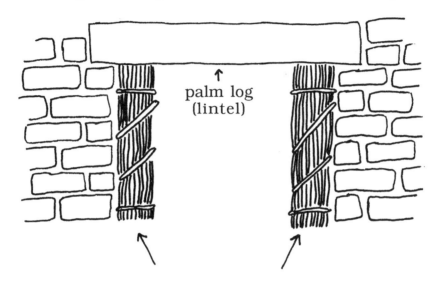

palm log
(lintel)

papyrus stalks bundled together
(posts)

Have students observe the ways the post-and-lintel method is used in architecture today.

Foundation for Architecture, Philadelphia

53. THE CORBELLED ARCH

A corbelled arch is not a true arch. It is really a series of cantilevers that are staggered inwards and are supported by the weight of the other stones or bricks above them. It was an early method used to span the openings in a wall (doors or windows).

Books can easily be stacked to form a corbelled arch.

Ancient earth tombs and contemporary igloos use the principle of corbelling to make round dome-like structures.

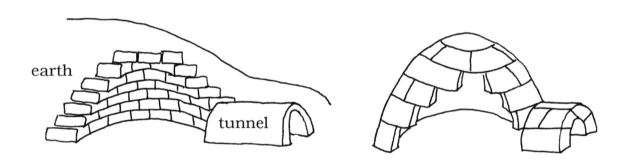

earth

tunnel

K-12   **S • SS • LA • A**

Foundation for Architecture, Philadelphia

54. THE ARCH AND KEYSTONE

A true arch is a curving structure that can span an opening in a wall. It is made from wedge-shaped pieces (voussoirs) that lean against each other (in compression). The central piece is often larger than the others. It is called the keystone, and is the last piece to be put into place. An arch made in this way is put into place supported by a scaffold, which is then removed.

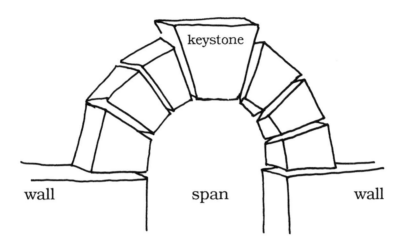

wall   span   wall

TO CONSTRUCT:

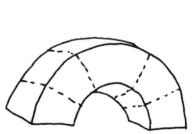

Out of styrofoam or florists' foam, use a sharp knife to cut an arch.

Slice out wedges (voussoirs). Be sure that keystone has a vertical axis.

A curved piece of construction paper will support the voussoirs until the keystone is placed.

(Challenge: Find out why Pennsylvania is called the Keystone State.)

K-12   **S • SS • LA • A**

Foundation for Architecture, Philadelphia

55. THE BUTTRESS

A buttress is a thickening in a wall to make it stronger, or small outside walls at right angles acting to counteract the outward thrust of a heavy roof or wall.

Buildings on hillsides often have buttresses pushing up against the down-hill wall.

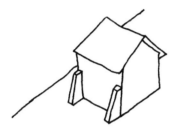 

56. THE FLYING BUTTRESS

A flying buttress is a buttress with the non-structural part removed, giving a feeling of lightness. Gothic cathedrals relied heavily on flying buttresses.

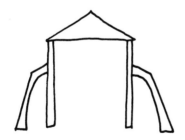 

4-12　　　　　　　　　　　　　　　**S • SS • LA • A**

Foundation for Architecture, Philadelphia

57. TRIANGULATION

Challenge students to try to hold up a book with one piece of construction paper. Show students that folding the paper (like an accordion) into a series of triangles will make it strong enough to hold more than one book. Given some experimentation, see how many books students can support with their paper.

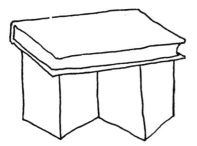

wide fold works
best this way

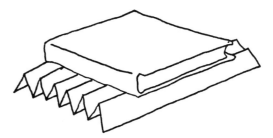

narrow fold works
best this way

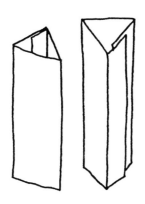

triangle columns

folded paper can make
a simple bridge

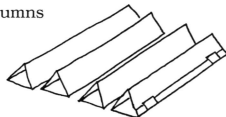

triangle beams

Foundation for Architecture, Philadelphia

58. THE TRUSS

A truss is a system of support members that are held rigid; i.e., will not tend to collapse with the addition of a load. Have students investigate truss forms using tongue depressors that have small holes drilled in the ends and are joined with paper fasteners.

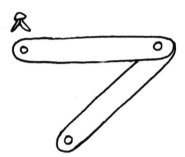

Students must find a way to join the tongue depressors into rigid shapes, shapes that will not change. After some experimenting, the class should come to see that the TRIANGLE is the only shape that fulfills this requirement.

A truss tends to be a series of triangles. Trusses can be found in bridges, pylons for electrical cables, or the Eiffel Tower.

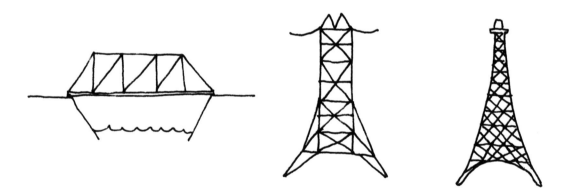

Students will find that what seem to be interconnections of squares and triangles will almost always break down into triangles, as a diagonal brace will be added to a rectangular shape to keep it rigid.

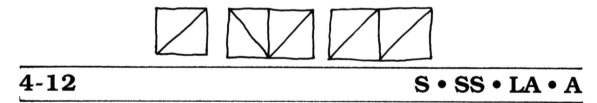

4-12   **S • SS • LA • A**

Foundation for Architecture, Philadelphia

59. TOOTHPICK AND MARSHMALLOW CONSTRUCTION

Hand out to each student about fifty colored toothpicks and thirty small marshmallows. (Marshmallows may be sprayed with hairspray so that students will not eat them). Each student is to use these materials to make any kind of structure; they must try to use all of their toothpicks and they may NOT STOP for a specific amount of time (10-15 minutes).

Compare the final results. Find out which structures are the most stable and see if students can deduct that the most stable form is based on a system of triangles. Show slides of trussing (Eiffel Tower, radio towers, etc.) and focus on the build-up of triangles.

Have students repeat the exercise; make specific guidelines for:

> ... the highest structure
> ... the widest or largest in all directions
> ... the smallest structure
> ... the most stable structure

3-12   **S • M • LA • A**

Additional rules may be developed: each marshmallow can only have four toothpicks piercing it, the structure must use thirty toothpicks and fifteen marshmallows, etc., to see what kinds of forms will be generated.

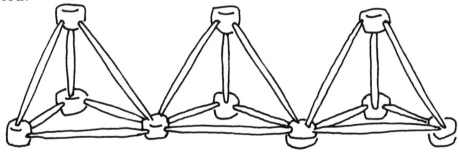

A dome-like structure can be covered with plastic wrap to make a terrarium.

Follow up on a larger scale with newspaper logs.

6-12   **S • M • SS • LA • A**

Foundation for Architecture, Philadelphia

60. NEWSPAPER LOG CONSTRUCTIONS

Students roll newspaper sections (lengthwise) into "logs" and tape tightly around the middle. Each student should make at least ten; the more, the better. Using tape as joints (have several rolls on hand, at least one roll for every two students), groups work together to make a structure big enough for a person to get into. Excellent to illustrate the principles of:

Beams • Columns • Frames • Trusses • Triangulation

Extend or join structures to form a space big enough for the whole group to get inside.

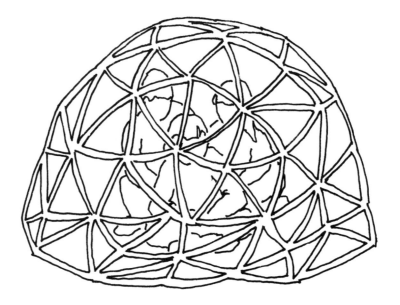

4-12   **S • M • SS • LA • A**

Foundation for Architecture, Philadelphia

61. THE DOME

A dome (from Latin *domus*, home) is a three dimensional form based on a circle. A dome may be half of a sphere, but can take many other shapes.

Explain that the structure of a dome is a series of equal **arches** that span the circle and meet in the center. These arches are called the **ribs**, just like the bones in students' chest cavities that **support** their upper bodies, give **shape** to their torsos, and **protect** their lungs.

Have students make a dome frame out of pipe cleaners. They will see that the arches need to be fixed with rings (as a barrel is), so that the dome won't collapse under a load.

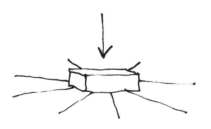

The top of a dome is in compression, and gets stronger under a load because the ribs are pressed against each other. The bottom of the dome is in tension, because the ribs want to push away from each other. The bottom ring will prevent this.

Foundation for Architecture, Philadelphia

An egg shell is two domes put together; one end is narrower than the other. Egg shells are surprisingly strong. Demonstrate by supporting books with 4 halved egg shell ends. Egg cartons follow the shape of the eggs because of the natural strength of the form, and provide a series of equal domes that can be used for demonstrations. Place a board on an egg carton and see if it will support a person's weight.

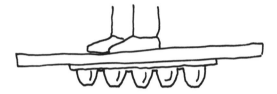

K-12 **S • M • SS • LA • A**

A **geodesic** dome gets its name from the Greek words for "earth-dividing" because it is a half-sphere divided into triangles. Students can make geodesic models using toothpick/marshmallow construction, straws with pipe cleaner joints, or newspaper logs.

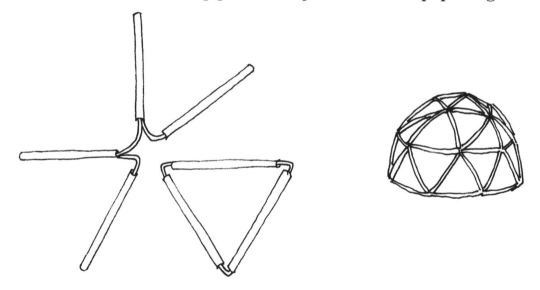

Covered with clear plastic, a small geodesic dome can become a miniature greenhouse.

4-12 **S • M • SS • LA • A**

Foundation for Architecture, Philadelphia

62. THE STRUCTURAL FRAME: SHOEBOX CUTAWAY

Each student will bring to class a shoebox. Using scissors, ask students to cut away all parts of the box that are non-structural; that is, that are not necessary to maintain the basic (rectangular) shape of the original box. Students should eventually end up with a "skeleton" or "frame" of the box:

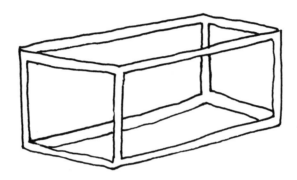

This frame is useful to illustrate the frames used in buildings. Visit a construction site to see how a building looks before the walls are added.

The frame can be "built up" again into a room or building by adding paper walls, roof, floor, etc. Emphasize that these added elements are non-structural, as they do not support the basic shape but are supported by it.

4-12   **S • M • SS • LA • A**

On a neighborhood walk, have students choose a building and draw an "x-ray" of it, showing how they imagine its structural frame, or skeleton, might look.

(Classes in the Philadelphia area should visit the "Ghost House," a steel frame that shows the probable shape of Benjamin Franklin's home.)

4-12   **S • M • SS • LA • A**

63. MODELS OF MODULES

Show slides of buildings made out of modules (pre-made forms that are connected together).

Using the following patterns, students will make paper module shapes of cubes and pyramids; the bases are **congruent** to facilitate easy combinations when glued together. Young students might be limited to two or three modules; older student will be able to make the modules more quickly and will have access to more complicated forms.

To decorate, use clear tape to form modules and have students plan their structures. They will use pencils to indicate their decorations (facade motifs, designs, patterns). Slit the tape and splay the form out flat to develop the decoration; reassemble.

The results may be arranged into a model community; some students may want to connect their constructions to others, forming high-rise structures.

Point out that the advantage of a modular construction is that parts can be added constantly. Compare to a honeycomb.

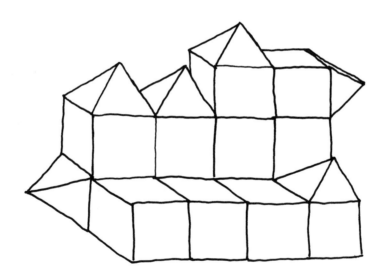

4-12   **S • M • SS • LA • A**

64. CUBE MODULE PATTERN

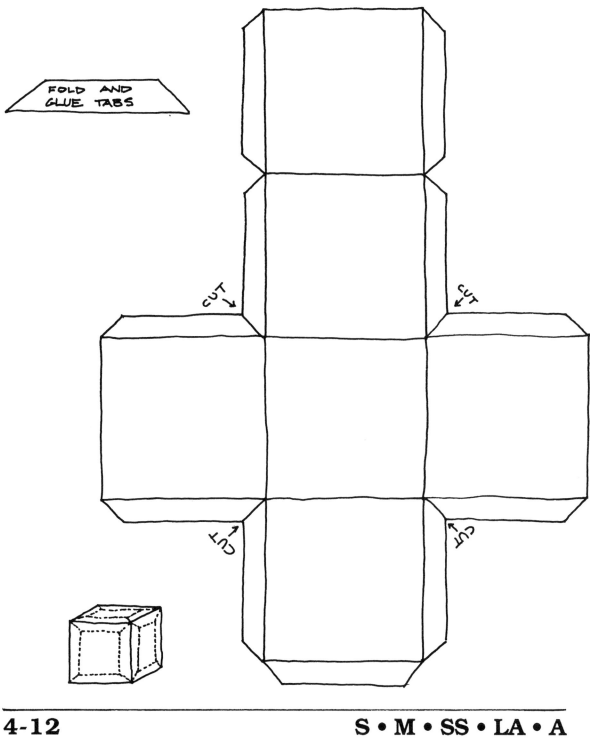

FOLD AND GLUE TABS

CUT

CUT

CUT

CUT

4-12

S • M • SS • LA • A

Foundation for Architecture, Philadelphia

65. PYRAMID MODULE PATTERN

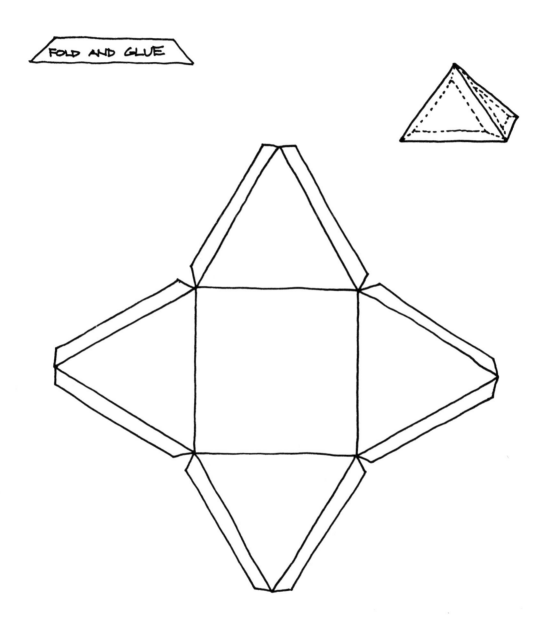

FOLD AND GLUE

S • M • SS • LA • A

Foundation for Architecture, Philadelphia

66. BRIDGES

The subject of bridge building is so all-encompassing that many books have been published devoted to this specific topic. Issues for study include:

- history of technology and materials

- structures

- geography, topology and geology of bridge sites

- transportation and communication

- city growth and planning; overcoming natural boundaries

- importance in military strategy

In keeping with the paradigm "form follows function", a bridge expresses its purpose and technology with a clarity and elegance often obscured in other types of structures. Bridge constructions offer a "bare-bones" look at structural considerations as the "skeleton" is often left visible.

There are many different kinds of bridges:

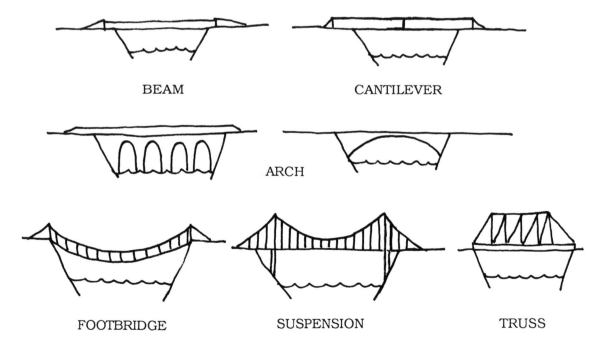

BEAM   CANTILEVER

ARCH

FOOTBRIDGE   SUSPENSION   TRUSS

Foundation for Architecture, Philadelphia

Students can experience some of the forces acting on bridges through physical demonstrations:

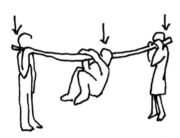

Students supporting the ends of the beam will feel the downward push. A long beam will sag in the middle when enough weight is applied, and would eventually break. A truss would hold the beam rigid so that the weight of the load would be evenly distributed.

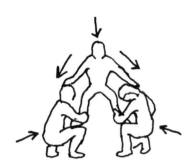

Students who support an arch will feel the weight pushing down and out. Acting as **abutments** (akin to buttresses), they will tend to lean inwards to counteract this thrust. All three students are feeling compressive forces.

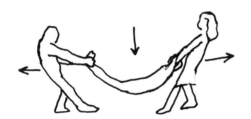

Students acting as a suspension bridge will feel themselves stretched in reaction to the load. The supporting students will lean out to counteract the downward thrust. All three students are in tension.

Students can use different materials to span distances between desks. Demonstrate how much more likely a material is to sag when the span is increased. Use paper clips to span a distance; they will indicate the shape of a **catenary arch,** which is often used as part of a curving truss.

4-12   **S • M • SS • LA • A**

Foundation for Architecture, Philadelphia

67. FOUNDATIONS

As a chain is only as strong as its weakest link, so a building is only as strong as its foundation. Take two activity periods to introduce students to the importance of a building's foundation.

In the first session, provide the class with a variety of materials and ask them to use these materials to make a small-scale structure. The only limitation is time. Suggested materials:

popsicle sticks	styrofoam or plastic cups
tongue depressors	pipe cleaners
dowels	corrugated cardboard
tooth picks	latex glue
straws	clay
corks	string and yarn (lashing)

A half-hour or forty-five minutes should be enough time for students to have some form of construction; these structures do not have to be "finished" for the demonstration to be clear. Students now take their models outside to an area where a hose and faucet and a natural ground surface are available. The purpose of the demonstration is to show how water will "wash away" a building that is not somehow embedded firmly in the ground. Place the models on a grassy or dirt-covered area and ask students which structures they think might be able to withstand even the lightest pressure of the water; you can safely assume that none of the students will have considered this issue in their models. Turn on the hose using light pressure and show how the water pushes the structures aside.

Discuss with students the various possibilities for fixing their structures firmly to the ground. (Putting a heavy rock inside a structure for ballast will "work" on this scale but is obviously not a solution that can be translated into the real world.) Show illustrations from *Underground* (Macaulay) to explain the advantage of embedding a building's foundation solidly into the ground.

For the second stage of the activity, have students make a second structure which will undergo the same treatment as the first one. Allow more time; students might work on this project at home, and be given an opportunity to dig out a "basement" in the designated area. If the students have understood the principles involved, their second model should include a "sub-structure" of piers or supports that will embed the model into the ground. The models should now be able to withstand the same or even an increased degree of water pressure. Pictures of the devastation caused by hurricanes, mud slides, monsoons and typhoons will dramatically illustrate the forces of water and wind on structures.

4-12   **S • M • SS • LA • A**

68. SUGGESTIONS FOR FOUNDATIONS

The simplest solution to the students' problem is to affix sturdy piers to their structures that can be stuck well into the ground. Students might also dig down into the surface and imbed globs or walls of clay, which can better grip the piers. A very elaborate solution, and one that best parallels actual building methods, would be to dig trenches and pour in plaster (as a substitute for cement); piers must be embedded quickly before the plaster hardens. A plaster foundation will be able to withstand extreme water pressure.

Another solution is to raise the model up on "stilts", as dwellings in the rain forest or other heavily flooded areas are elevated to let water pass below the shelter itself. Even in this case the base posts must be well anchored and can be stabilized at ground level with rocks or clay.

Take note of the ground itself; is it very sandy or is there a high natural clay content? How does this affect the solution?

Take your class to a construction site when the foundation will still be apparent. Consecutive visits will increase their awareness of the foundation's importance and also illustrate many of the structural principles that they have studied.

4-12   **S • M • SS • LA • A**

69. TENTS AS "PRIMITIVE" STRUCTURES

Use commercially made tents to illustrate structural principles. Have students bring tents to school, or better yet, take your class on an overnight camping trip. Although for actual sleeping comfort you may want to take advantage of a campsite with cabins available, encourage students who have access to tents to bring them, and assign teams to set them up. Have the students make note (drawings) of the structures (poles, lines and stakes) that support the tent. Tents are an excellent illustration of the "skeleton" (supports) and "skin" (fabric) of a structure. Discuss the different materials used, and weigh the relative merits of wood, fiberglass, canvas and nylon.

flexibility	water repellance	insulation
rigidity	air passage (breathing)	weight
stability	wind resistance	interior or exterior skeleton

Discuss:

- How are the joints fastened?
- Where are the greatest areas of stress?
- How is the tent stabilized?
- Which tent lets the most air in? Light?
- Which tent is the heaviest? Lightest? How would the tent's weight affect its use?
- Why would some cultures live in tents all the time, when other people build solid, immovable homes?

4-12   **S • M • SS • LA**

Foundation for Architecture, Philadelphia

70. ROUGHING IT

For a more adventurous camping project, have students construct shelters out of raw materials found around the campsite.

The simplest shelter is merely a shelter for the upper body constructed over the head end of a sleeping bag. A larger lean-to structure offers more shelter from wind and morning moisture. Young, flexible trees close together can be (gently!) lashed together and covered with blankets to form a teepee (the trees must not be harmed and must be unlashed when you leave). Students can use sticks to make smaller models of structures with broad leaves woven in to make roofs and walls. Large trees with protruding roots and low thick branches or dense foliage can offer a rudimentary natural shelter; look for promising rock formation or shallow caves. The more time you can spend developing these natural shelters, the more issues you can discuss.

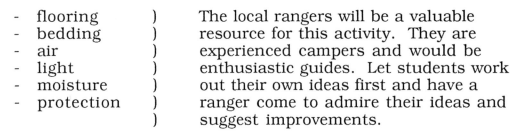

- flooring	)	The local rangers will be a valuable
- bedding	)	resource for this activity. They are
- air	)	experienced campers and would be
- light	)	enthusiastic guides. Let students work
- moisture	)	out their own ideas first and have a
- protection	)	ranger come to admire their ideas and
	)	suggest improvements.

Students will naturally hit upon many of the problems and solutions faced by "primitive" cultures. Back in class, show slides of dwellings from rain forests, deserts and of American Indian dwellings so that students can see the similarities between those structures and their own. If you build a fire with students, remember that architectural principles are also at work there. Again, take advantage of the park rangers, who can show students many different "building techniques". If you use a ready-made fireplace, discuss with students the structural principles, the design, and the materials used. A fireplace offers a clear illustration of suction and air circulation as smoke is drawn up the chimney and vented away from the fire.

6-12   **S • M • SS • LA**

Foundation for Architecture, Philadelphia

71. AMERICAN INDIAN TEEPEES

Use sticks or dowels to make a frame that can be embedded in a clay base. Hold the dowels together at the top with thread.

Students will cut a semi-circular shape of paper to be decorated with appropriate Indian motifs, and then wrapped around the frame.

K-4   **SS • LA • A**

72. AMERICAN INDIAN PUEBLOS

A modular pueblo village can be constructed using clay slabs supported at the top by thin wood dowels, which parallel their actual construction. Popsicle sticks may be embedded in the clay walls for support, and also to help maintain a consistent scale. Or, clay or sandpaper can be used to cover a support structure cut from various sizes of milk cartons. Use toothpicks, sticks, or straws to make ladders from one level to the next.

K-4   **SS • LA • A**

73. VOCABULARY: STRUCTURES

arch
A-frame
abut
abutment
anchor

balance
buttress
beam
  I-beam
  H-beam
balloon frame
brace
base

ceiling
column
compression
construct, construction
counteract
corner
carpenter's tools
catenary arch
catenary curve
collapse
corbel
corbelled arch
Corinthian capital
colonnade
cantilever
counter balance
counter thrust
corrugate

dome
Doric capital
dead weight
dimension

equalize
erosion

frame
flying buttress
foundation
floor
force

geodesic dome
gravity

horizontal
height

Ionic capital

joist
joint
joyce

keystone

load
load bearing
load bearing floor
lean-to
lintel
live load

module
mass
measurement

non-structural

pillar
post and lintel
pilaster
pier
plumb
pile, piling
pressure

rib
rigid
rafter
roof
resistance

structure
structural
shape
skeleton
sub-structure
support
suspension
stable, stability
skin
span
stress
sag
stud
strut
scaffold

tunnel
triangle, triangulation
tension
truss
thrust

vertical
vault
volume
voussoir

weight
weight distribution
wall board
wind resistance
wall
width

Foundation for Architecture, Philadelphia

HOME

Home is usually the student's most intimate contact with the built environment. These exercises are grouped together to provide introductory activities that do not require specialized vocabulary.

HOME

74. WHAT IS YOUR FAVORITE PLACE?

Tell your students that you would like them to take some silent time
to think about their favorite places. Do not define "place"; it can be
inside or outside, in the natural or in the built environment. Have your
students close their eyes in order to fix their images clearly in their
minds. Speak slowly and softly, and give them time to giggle and
relax. Without rushing, ask a series of specific questions to help them
develop their mental images; the questions are not to be answered
aloud.

- Are you inside or outside?
- What time of day or night is it?
- Is it light or dark?
- What do you see there?
- What colors do you see?
- What can you hear?
- What smells can you remember?
- Can you taste anything there?
- What can you touch?
- Are you there alone, or is anyone else there? (Maybe
  there are animals or birds around.)
- How does this place make you feel?
- What do you do while you are there?
- How do you get there?

Take up to five minutes for this part of the activity. Notice that at no
time are the students asked to name their places. Explain to them
that now they will answer these questions on paper, and that they are
going to try to guess each other's places based on their descriptions,
so they must NOT name the place out loud!

Hand out a list of the questions to each student; add any that might be
appropriate. Point out that they must think about the **five senses** as
they write: **sight**, **hearing**, **smell**, **taste**, and **touch**. They will also
include the emotions that they experience there.

Once the students have finished writing, give them a piece of drawing
paper the same size as the paper they have written on (for display);
ask them to draw a picture of their place, including as much as they
can remember. They will write the name of the place on the drawing.

K-12   **SS • LA • A**

Foundation for Architecture, Philadelphia

75. WHAT IS YOUR ROOM LIKE?

Have students write a description of their own rooms. They should describe the room itself in terms of color, shape, window, doors and closets; furniture; people who share the room; what they do there; associated feelings.

Give each student a piece of oak tag cut so that it will fold into an open-topped cube or rectangle that approximates their rooms.

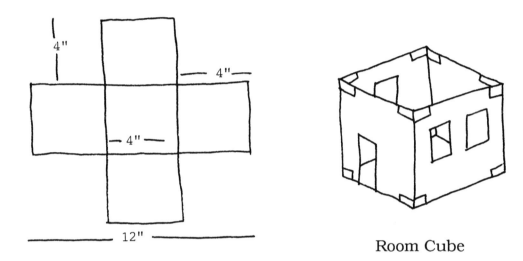

Room Cube

Have the students draw the four sides of their rooms onto the four sides of the paper; doors and windows may be cut out.

Fold up and tape into a box. (Scoring the paper on the opposite side of the fold will give a sharp crease. Shoeboxes can be used instead, but the "walls" should be covered in white paper to make the drawings legible.)

Students will present and explain their models to the class.

3-12   **SS • LA • A**

76. DRAW YOUR FIRST HOME

Acting as a model for your students, visualize the first home you can remember and make a drawing of it. Use your memories and this picture to stimulate a discussion with your students of their first homes, or the first homes that they can remember. Help students visualize by having them close their eyes and tell a partner what they "see". Next, have students brainstorm their ideas by writing words and phrases of their memories on one side of a piece of white drawing paper. On the other side, they will draw and color the picture they have developed. Last, have the students organize their thoughts into a coherent, descriptive essay. The memories should develop and increase through these steps; encourage students to try to revive smells, sounds, tastes, and tactile experiences associated with this early home, as well as neighbors, emotional experiences, or any other memory which can be expressed, either visually or in words.

This activity is especially effective for a class with a large transient (military) or immigrant population, as it gives students a chance to share diverse backgrounds. If there is a large proportion of students from a specific area (Asia, Europe, Africa, South or Central America), show slides of buildings and homes from that area to help those students flesh out their memories and express them to the rest of the class.

Students who have always lived in the same home can generate early memories, and think about ways their homes have changed, or complete the activity using memories of a relative's or friend's home.

4-12   **SS • LA • A**

77. DRAW YOUR PRESENT HOME FROM MEMORY

Introduce this activity using the word "home" instead of "house" to avoid discomfort for students who live in apartments or projects. Help students visualize by having them close their eyes and tell a partner what they "see". Independent writers will brainstorm a list of words and phrases of what they can remember on one side of a piece of white drawing paper. They will draw this image on the other side. If students get "stuck", reassure them that hardly anyone can remember familiar things perfectly and that the fun of this activity is to see how much we forget! You might also talk a student through an image by asking specific questions. (What color is your front door? Does it have a window in it?); do not draw pictures for them, as they may rely on your images instead of their own memories.

K-12   **SS • LA • A**

For homework, students take another piece of drawing paper home to make a drawing "on site". They should take note of the elements they forgot and write those on one side of the paper, then make the second picture. In class, students will compare their drawings, which will make an interesting display.

Students can organize the words and phrases they have written into a descriptive essay about their homes. Encourage them to include smells, sounds, tactile and emotion experiences.

NOTE ON SAFETY: Especially in lower grades, a letter should go home to parents that students will be drawing their homes on site, in case any students live on busy streets and would require supervision, or should take an alternate view.

3-12   **SS • LA • A**

78. WRITE ABOUT YOUR HOME

Students can use the following questionnaire (K-3 or students with undeveloped writing skills may dictate the answers to an adult) to gather specific information about their homes. This information can become the basis for a descriptive essay or poem that should include reference to their five senses as well as emotional feelings associated with different places in their homes.

K-6   **SS • LA • A**

79. MY HOME: QUESTIONNAIRE

THE OUTSIDE:

My home is _____ stories high. It is made out of _____.

Its colors are _____. There are _____

windows and _____ doors in my home. The front door is made of

_____. The front door is _____ feet by _____.

Some of the other things on the front of my home are _____

_____. Some of the things in my

yard are : _____.

The roof of my home has this shape (draw):

It is covered with _____. The chimney is located

_____.

THE INSIDE:

There are _____ rooms in my home. The largest room is the

_____. The smallest room is the _____.

The kitchen floor is made of _____. The bathroom

floor is made of _____. There are _____ stairways

in my home. The total number of steps is _____. I can see

these things from my bedroom window: _____

_____. My favorite room is

_____. The things in this room are _____

_____.

K-6   **SS • LA**

Foundation for Architecture, Philadelphia

80. WHAT'S OUTSIDE YOUR FRONT DOOR?

As a homework project, students will develop a labelled drawing of the environment in front of their homes. This will be an example of a view drawn in the form of an architectural **section**, or side view. (Students should use a back or side entrance if it is safer or more accessible.)

The drawing should include:

- one doorway and its elements
- the surrounding environment (yard, sidewalk, streets, etc.)
- the reasons for and functions of the elements (lighting for safety and night visibility, flowers for decorations, etc.)
- qualities and associated feelings (dark, creepy place under the front porch, the mailbox where I get letters, streets where I'm not allowed to play in traffic, wall with messy grafitti, etc.)
- reference to each of the five senses
    - 5 colors
    - 5 materials
    - 3 noises
    - 2 smells

Students will use these drawings to develop a poem or essay to describe "A Walk Up To My Front Door".

Foundation for Architecture, Philadelphia

81. INSIDE AND OUTSIDE: WINDOWS AT HOME

Have students draw their windows at home. They should show the view both from the outside **in** and from the inside **out**.

WHAT'S <u>INSIDE</u> MY WINDOWS?   **WHAT'S <u>OUTSIDE</u> MY WINDOWS?**

(Students will have to imagine
what they might see if they
could look inside all of the
windows.)

Young students can complete this activity at home with an adult.

NOTE ON SAFETY: Send a note home to alert parents that children will be looking out of windows; tell children to draw an outside view by standing two steps back from the window.

K-12   **SS • A**

Foundation for Architecture, Philadelphia

82. ENERGY SYSTEMS AT HOME

Have students investigate the energy systems in their homes. Encourage parents to help students fill out this form.

1. The Electrical System
Can you find the electrical panel box?_____ Where is it located? _____ What do you think it does? _____ What carries the electricity from the panel box to the lights and outlets in your home? _____ _____ What device turns the electricity "on" or "off"? _____.

2. The Plumbing System
The plumbing system is made up of two "loops". One loop supplies fresh, clean water. The other loop takes the used, dirty water away, out of the house. Can you find the main water service in your house? _____ Where is it? _____ Can you find the sewage waste water pipe? _____ Where is it located? _____ Do you see any copper-colored pipes? _____ These supply clean water to the various "fixtures" in your home - the sinks, bathtubs, and so on. Can you find the water heater? _____ What fuel does it use? _____

3. The Heating System
How is heat delivered to your bedroom? (Radiator, register, baseboard, heater, space heater) _____. How can you control how much heat is supplied to your room? _____ Can you find the furnace/boiler for your house? _____ What fuel does it use? _____

3-12   **S • SS • LA**

Foundation for Architecture, Philadelphia

83. HOME MAINTENANCE

Parents can become involved with their children's projects by discussing with them the many responsibilities involved in home maintenance. (Be careful to avoid making a distinction between home owners and renting families; be sensitive to the fact that renters do not have the same freedom of choice as owners do.) All families bear the burdens of repairs, utility bills, and conservation of energy and resources. Students can become knowledgeable partners in many of these issues as they learn the financial and ecological consequences of their behavior at home. Discuss with students the reasons for:

- turning off lights and faucets when not in use
- using cold water to wash clothes
- closing outside doors and windows promptly in the winter
- closing the refrigerator door promptly
- cleaning up spills quickly to avoid stains
- keeping the thermostat lowered in winter
- installing insulation
- keeping food and garbage covered or put away
- controlling animals

K-12   S • SS • LA

Students can measure various volumes of water and use multiplication skills to determine the quantities of water used over a particular time span.

- Based on the number of gallons your toilet tank holds, how much water is used to flush the toilet 10 times a day?
- Based on the amount of water your bathtub holds, how much water is used if 3 people take baths? Compare the amount of water used for a shower by closing the drain during a shower.
- Extend to: washing machine, kitchen sink, dishwashing machine, etc.

4-12   S • M • SS

84. IMAGINE YOUR "DREAM HOUSE"

Have students imagine that they can design any sort of building for themselves to live in.

First they will write an imaginative essay that answers specific questions about the building.

- Where would it be?

- What would it look like?

- What would it be made out of?

- How big would it be?

- How many rooms?

- How would you use the rooms?

- What kind of furniture or equipment would you like to have?

- Would anyone else live there? Pets?

Once the students have developed this fantasy in words, they will draw a picture of it, including the outside environment. They may use color and applique to flesh out their images.

Once students have developed a vocabulary and learned some planning techniques, they can continue with this image and develop a model, as in EXTERIORS.

K-12   **SS • LA • A**

85. VOCABULARY: ENERGY AT HOME

air conditioner
air pocket
awning
baseboard
chimney
circulation
curtain
draft
drapes
duct
electricity
fan
flue
frozen pipes
furnace
gas, natural gas
gasoline
gauge
heat
heater
heat loss
insulation
louver
meter (oil, gas, water)
pipes
radiator
register
screen
seal
shade
shutter
solar
storm doors
storm windows
switch
system
temperature
thermal windows
thermostat
valve
venetian blinds
vent
ventilation

Foundation for Architecture, Philadelphia

INTERIORS

These activities help students articulate their responses to aspects of interior design and also explain some of the professional architect's working methods.

INTERIORS

86. WHAT DO DIFFERENT INTERIORS "FEEL" LIKE?

Choose two different areas, either in the classroom or using areas in other parts of the school, where you can make temporary changes.

Exaggerate a specific aspect of each area by rearranging furniture, changing the lighting and wall decor, etc. For example, in a carpeted area, bring comfortable chairs, put pillows around, hang a pleasant picture, play soft music on a radio, and soften the lights to make it as comfortable and "homey" as possible.

In contrast, place uncomfortable-looking chairs far apart from each other in an uncarpeted space with no windows and no wall decoration.

Take students to each space, and generate a discussion about the "feel" or "atmosphere" (ambience) of each space. Generate a list of descriptive adjectives, metaphors and similies made by the students; generate a parallel list of what specific aspects give each space its particular ambience.

Emphasize the **five senses**.

K-12   **SS • LA**

After the above exercise, read vivid passages from various literary selections to the students; compare the author's word use and metaphors to their own.

K-12   **SS • LA**

Have the students choose a room or space and write a description which focusses on an emotional effect and makes specific mention of at least four senses. (The sense of taste is the most difficult one to evoke in this context.)

4-12   **SS • LA**

87. WHAT'S IN A ROOM?

Ask students how they would define a "room". (A room is usually assumed to have floor, walls and ceiling which define it, as well as a particular **function** that sets it apart from other rooms.)

How do we get from one room to another? (The issue of doorways, doors, halls and passageways is crucial for later work in FLOORPLANS; remember that an interior door always serves two rooms at once.)

Are there often windows between rooms? Why? Brainstorm a list of the different kinds of rooms (vocabulary list follows.) What are the special functions of these rooms? What activities take place in each one?

From the list, choose five and extend discussion of their special qualities in terms of:

- function
- public or private use (in a home, "public" can mean guests while "private" means limited to family use as well as individuals)
- furniture (characterize furniture; a kitchen stool is very different from an arm chair)
- size (relative to other rooms in the building)
- materials
- windows (why are they important?)

K-12   **SS • LA**

Have students write a description of a walk through their homes; they must mention each room and hallway and mention at least two unique characteristics of each room. (Unenclosed porches can be very interesting as they include aspects of a defined room yet have either thin or open walls, making them part of the inside of the house and part of the outdoors at the same time.)

4-12   **SS • LA**

---

88. VOCABULARY: INTERIORS

Types of Rooms	Architectural Elements of Rooms
alcove	archway
ante-room	bannister
attic	baseboard
ballroom	carpet
basement	carpet-padding
bedroom	chandelier
cafeteria	column
carport	curtain
cellar	counter
chamber	dimensions
closet	door knob
conservatory	doorway
crawl space	drapes, drapery
den	duct
dining room	elevator
drawing room	escalator
dressing room	fireplace
entrance	floor
foyer	furniture
garage	lamp
half-bathroom	lighting
hall	mezzanine
kitchen	mirror
library	moulding
living room	outlet
lobby	panelling
nook	parquet
nursery	partition
office	rafter
pantry	rug
rec(reation) room	screen
root cellar	shelves
sitting room	spiral stairway
stairway	stairway
study	upholstery
sun room	wainscoting
verandah	wall
vestibule	wall paper
	window; sash, shade, sill

K-12   **SS • LA**

Foundation for Architecture, Philadelphia

89. FURNITURE DESIGN

Brainstorm with students a list of different kinds of furniture; categorize the items in the list according to broad categories (tables, chairs, beds, cabinets, shelves, etc.) and discuss the need for variation. I.e., how and why is a kitchen chair different from a stuffed armchair? How and why is a desk different from a coffee table? Include aspects such as materials, structure, appearance, and portability. Students may use pipe cleaners and assorted materials to design and arrange furniture for a specific use in a specific room and should be able to give reasons for their design choices.

Show slides of a wide variety of types and styles; let students speculate as to the function, ownership, time period and culture behind the furniture.

K-12   **SS • LA • A**

90. VOCABULARY: FURNITURE

bed
  - crib
  - trundle bed
  - twin, queen, king size
  - bunk bed
  - cot
  - Murphy bed

chair
  - easy chair
  - arm chair
  - recliner
  - stool
  - high chair
  - wing-back chair
  - straight-back chair
  - kitchen chair
  - dining room chair
  - throne

couch
  - sofa
  - love seat
  - bench
  - pew

table
  - dining room table
  - kitchen table
  - coffee table
  - end table
  - work table
  - desk

cabinet, closet, shelves
  - wardrobe
  - chiffarobe
  - cedar closet
  - chest
  - hutch
  - sideboard
  - dresser
  - bureau
  - chest of drawers
  - book shelves
  - kitchen cabinet

K-12   **SS • LA**

91. THE SOCIAL DYNAMICS OF FURNITURE ARRANGEMENT

Have the students think about the reasons for furniture placement and its effects. Observe with them the regular arrangement of desks, tables, chairs, shelving and blackboards in their classroom. Discuss the probable reasons for the structure (i.e. students facing teacher = lecture). Rearrange the furniture to see how group dynamics change (chairs in a circle facing towards center = discussion; chairs facing away from each other = isolation; chairs spread around at different tables = individual study). Group the students in various ways to show how dynamics change (students grouped close together is appropriate for all to see a small display together but not good for getting work done). Encourage the students to suggest improvements in the classroom's arrangement.

Take students to parts of the school to discuss the different ways of arranging a space according to the specific activity. Why is a cafeteria arranged differently from the library, the gym, or the auditorium? How do the furnishings affect the social interactions? Can the students suggest improvements?

Have the students analyze the furniture in their homes. How does furniture in a kitchen differ from furniture in a living room? What if the refrigerator were in the bedroom, or the bathtub in a bedroom?

K-12   SS • LA

Have the students write a description of the furniture in a public space. How does the arrangement of the furniture affect the traffic flow? How does it control the human interactions? Does it separate people or join them together, or both?

6-12   SS • LA

Foundation for Architecture, Philadelphia

92. LIGHTING

Brainstorm with students the reasons for adequate light for human activities. It should soon be apparent that the list is endless. Point out the distinction between **natural** (sun) light and **artificial** light in the built environment. Students can make graphic indications of both kinds of light by using techniques of shading as they observe the lighting effects in a particular room under different circumstances. A drawing made at noon on a sunny day (no artificial lights) will be very different from the same room at night with one artificial light on. (If many lights are turned on at once, the lighting will become too complicated and subtle to record easily; the comparison will be more interesting if each light's effect is recorded by itself.)

4-12   **S • SS • LA •A**

Discuss with students the many ways that light can be changed in a room. Natural light can be controlled by curtains, shades, venetian blinds, shutters, and awnings. Artificial light can be controlled by the ON/OFF switch, lampshades, recessing lights, using different wattage. Have students find out which of these methods they can find at home and in school.

K-12   **S • SS • LA**

There are many potential topics for research in regard to lighting:

- lighting systems in history
- the invention, construction and operation of the lightbulb
- the difference between fluorescent and incandescent light
- the development and use of neon as a lighting source

6-12   **S • SS • LA**

93. ACOUSTICS

Introduce students to the importance of acoustics, or sound control, in the built environment. Take the class to a space in the school with bare walls, floor and ceiling, and little or no furniture. Compare the high noise level (perhaps with an echo, as in a gym) in this space with the low or "dead" noise level in a smaller space rich in textures which absorb sound; look for acoustic tiles on ceilings. Explain that sound waves bounce off of smooth, hard surfaces but are absorbed by soft, thick surfaces. See if the school library is a "quiet" room; note that the rows of books themselves will help absorb sound. Any performing musician could explain to students the difficulties of sound adjustments on stage and the difference between the acoustics in an empty hall as opposed to a hall filled with people. Ask students why so many people enjoy singing or whistling in the shower (the reflective effect of ceramic tile sharpens the human voice), or why it is so much fun to yell in an empty house. What is an echo? Why is it so often difficult to understand an announcer speaking through a microphone in a gymnasium? Under what circumstances should a room be "dead" (study room, bedroom, recording studio, auditorium)?

K-12   **S • SS • LA**

For research, have students investigate the etymologies of some of the words relating to acoustics. The origins of the words reflect the importance in ancient societies of building structures where many people could listen together to a political, social or artistic presentation.

- acoustic: Greek, *akoustikos* = hearing
- amphitheater: Greek, *amphi* = both; as, a place where sound is heard on both sides
- audible   )
  audience   ): Latin, *audire* = to hear
  audio   )
  auditorium)

Where do we find auditoriums today? What special structures and materials are used in auditoriums?

6-12   **S • SS• LA**

94. CLIMATE CONTROL

Have your class investigate the energy sources and systems of the school building to determine how a comfortable temperature (climate) is maintained in the school rooms.

First, go outside and determine the position of the school in terms of the sun. Establish the four cardinal directions (N, S, E, W). Which direction do the different walls of the school face? Which parts of the school get the most direct sunlight? Which parts get the least? This heat is **passive solar energy**; the rooms that get the most direct sunlight are the warmest rooms during the day and would be the most comfortable in the cold months. Which rooms would be the most comfortable in hot months? Which direction does your classroom face? Do students have any control over the temperature in the room (open or shut windows, venetian blinds, thermostat)?

K-12   **S • SS • LA**

95. ENERGY SYSTEMS AT SCHOOL

Make an appointment with a member of the maintenance staff who can give students a tour and explanation of the energy sources of the school building (plumbing, electricity, heating, air conditioning, waste disposal). Have students trace pipes, wiring, duct and vent systems. Discuss some of the expenses of the school's energy systems; let students guess at costs and compare to actual monetary figures.

David Macaulay's book *Underground* provides a graphic display of the subterranean interweavings of energy systems below a building; you may be able to trace your school's energy systems to find out where they connect to the city's sources by looking for vents and wires outside.

Students can use this introduction to help them trace the same elements at home.

K-12   **S • SS • LA**

Foundation for Architecture, Philadelphia

96. ROOM MATRICES

AREA	ACTIVITIES
LIVING ROOM	playing piano, radio, talking
DINING ROOM	homework, cards, meals
KITCHEN	meals, cooking, talking
BATHROOM	washing, toilet
BEDROOM #1	TV, sleeping, dressing
BEDROOM #2	sleeping, dressing, phone
BEDROOM #3	sleeping, dressing
BASEMENT	laundry, storage

ACTIVITIES

AREA \ TIME	6-8 am	8-10 am	10-12 am	12-2 pm	2-4 pm	4-6 pm	6-8 pm	8-10 pm	10-12 pm	12-6 am
LIVING	X					X				
DINING				X		X				
KITCHEN	X			X		X	X			
BATH	X				X			X	X	
BR #1	X							X		X
BR #2	X				X				X	X
BR #3	X									X
BASEMENT		X	X							

TIME USED

KEY: A - CLOSELY RELATED
B - SOMEWHAT RELATED
C - NO RELATION

LIVING
DINING
KITCHEN
BR #1
BR #2
BR #3
BATH
BASEMENT

SIMILARITY OF FUNCTION

FAMILY MEMBER \ AREA	LIVING	DINING	KITCHEN	BATH	BR 1	BR 2	BR 3	BASEMENT
FATHER	X	X	X	X	X			X
MOTHER	X	X	X	X	X			X
SISTER	X	X	X	X		X		
SELF	X	X	X	X			X	

PEOPLE

6-12

SS • LA

97. BUBBLE DIAGRAMS

A bubble diagram is an extremely simple visual description of the location of rooms on the same floor. It is appropriate for all age levels, as scale and passageways are not factors.

For older students, this is an excellent preliminary exercise for floor plans that depict a series of connecting rooms.

Students may make bubble diagrams of their homes, the school, or any other familiar place.

K-12   **M • SS • LA**

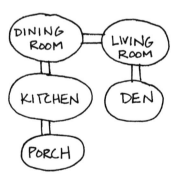

Lines from room to room are first indicators of passageways, i.e. doorways and halls that connect certain rooms. Scale is still not an important factor.

3-12   **M • SS • LA • A**

98. FLOOR PLANS

Floor plans are perhaps the most familiar image of the architect's profession. (They are often referred to as **blueprints** because of the method used in reproducing the architect's original drawing. This method is obsolete, but the use of the word is sure to remain in our language as a synonym for "plans".) Floor plans are **symbols** that represent an **aerial view** of the architectural elements of a structure. Professional architects use a standard code in their floor plans with regard to:

- the indications of dimensions
- scale
- symbols for construction features
- symbols for interior aspects (lighting, furniture, etc.)

Following is a generalized introduction to floor plans for use in the lower grades, or as a simplified explanation in upper grades. The symbols are given with an elevation of what the symbol represents, as the visualization from the aerial, two dimensional plan to the "upright" third dimension may present initial difficulties. Below is a reduction of the quiz with answers.

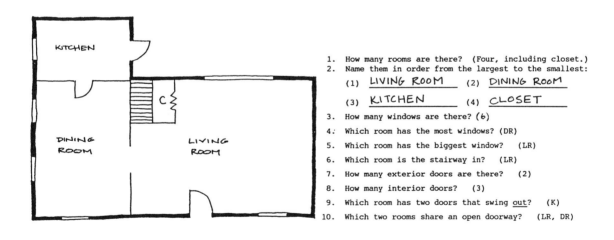

1. How many rooms are there? (Four, including closet.)
2. Name them in order from the largest to the smallest:

   (1) <u>LIVING ROOM</u>   (2) <u>DINING ROOM</u>

   (3) <u>KITCHEN</u>   (4) <u>CLOSET</u>

3. How many windows are there? (6)
4. Which room has the most windows? (DR)
5. Which room has the biggest window?   (LR)
6. Which room is the stairway in?   (LR)
7. How many exterior doors are there?   (2)
8. How many interior doors?   (3)
9. Which room has two doors that swing <u>out</u>?   (K)
10. Which two rooms share an open doorway?   (LR, DR)

Foundation for Architecture, Philadelphia

99. HOW TO READ A FLOOR PLAN

A floor plan is like a map of a room or a series of rooms. Like a map, it shows how a room would look from above, as if you were a bird flying overhead. An architect uses certain codes or symbols to explain the shapes and dimensions (sizes) of rooms, and also to explain where doors, windows, stairs, and furniture are.

WALLS:

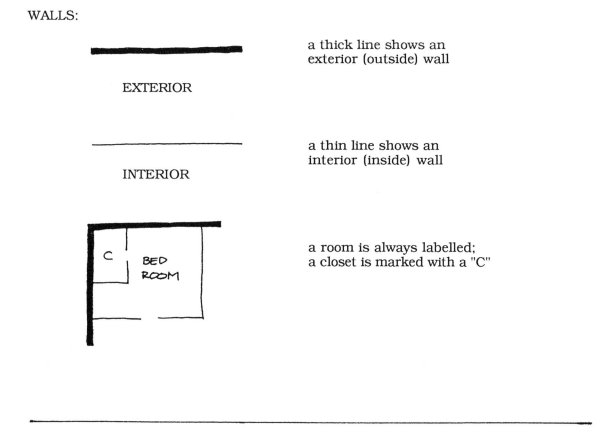

a thick line shows an exterior (outside) wall

EXTERIOR

a thin line shows an interior (inside) wall

INTERIOR

a room is always labelled; a closet is marked with a "C"

Foundation for Architecture, Philadelphia

DOORS
Some doorways are open: Spaces in a wall, with no door

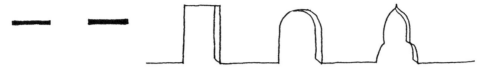

Some doors swing open and shut in one direction:

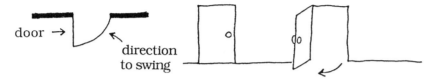

door →   ← direction to swing

Some doors fold open to each side:

Some doors fold up to one side like an accordion:

Some doors slide open and shut:

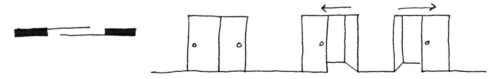

A door that moves in a circle is called a revolving door:

Foundation for Architecture, Philadelphia

Windows are shown by a double line in an exterior wall.

two narrow windows   one wide window

A staircase looks like steps seen from overhead.

Try to image what different kinds of furniture would look like from overhead. Here are some suggestions you can use.

lamp

tables with different shapes

a desk, chair and table lamp

armchair

tables with chairs

couch   bed   rug

a table on a rug with a couch and floor lamp

toilet   tub   sink   stove   refrigerator

Foundation for Architecture, Philadelphia

100. CAN YOU READ A FLOOR PLAN?

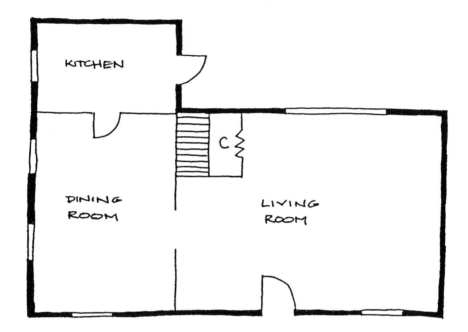

1. How many rooms are there?
2. Name them in order from the largest to the smallest:
    (1) _____   (2) _____
    (3) _____   (4) _____
3. How many windows are there?
4. Which room has the most windows?
5. Which room has the biggest window?
6. Which room is the stairway in?
7. How many exterior doors are there?
8. How many interior doors?
9. Which room has two doors that swing <u>out</u>?
10. Which two rooms share an open doorway?

Use the FURNITURE symbols to show how you would decorate these rooms. Remember not to put furniture at the bottom of the stairway or in front of a door.

3-8   **M • SS • LA • A**

101. FLOOR PLANS: NON-RECTANGULAR

Show slides that illustrate non-rectangular rooms (castles, tents, igloos, rooms with curved walls, teepees, etc). Have students draw a fantasy floor plan using a variety of shapes. Brainstorm geometric and irregular shapes for students to integrate into their plans.

Remind students that they must keep passageways in mind so that a person can get to every room. Tell students to "let your fingers do the walking" to see if all areas are accessible, or if more doors should be added. Have students notice that each interior wall serves two rooms at once, so that a change in one room makes a change in all bordering rooms.

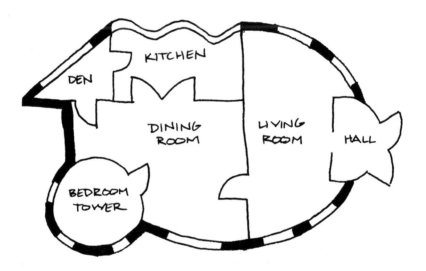

FANTASY HOUSE PLAN

4-12   **M • SS • LA • A**

Foundation for Architecture, Philadelphia

102. PLAN, SECTION, AND ELEVATION

Use a decorated paper cup to illustrate the meanings of an architectural plan, section, and elevation.

PLAN  SECTION  ELEVATION

- view from above (as in a map)

- a flat cross-section (cut the cup in half; outline the contour in black marker)

- an upright picture of one side

Have students project plans, sections and elevations for simply constructed objects. For plans, students should put the object on the floor and look down onto it. For a section, the student should draw only the outermost contour, trying to imagine what the object would look like if it were sliced through. The elevation will include exterior features, design, texture, etc.

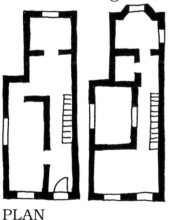 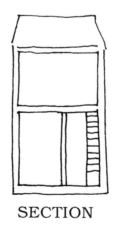 

PLAN SECTION ELEVATION

Foundation for Architecture, Philadelphia

103. FROM PLAN TO ELEVATION

Using oak tag or other stiff paper, give each student a piece to cut to approximate proportions so that it can eventually be folded and taped into an open-topped rectangle. (You can use a shoebox by slitting down each corner and tracing the splayed shape. The drawings should be made on paper and glued onto the shoebox, as the shoebox itself will not be a good drawing surface.)

On the center of the paper, which represents the floor, students will draw a **plan** of a familiar or invented room.

On the side parts, students will draw four **elevations** of the same room (a picture of each wall).

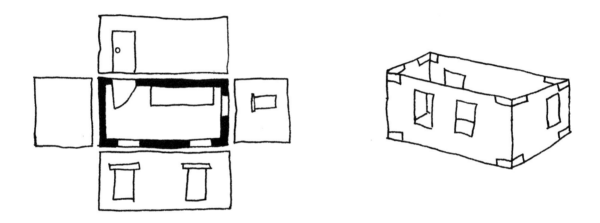

Once the boxes are reassembled, each wall should correspond to the indications on the floor. This activity will graphically help students understand the meaning of a plan and how it projects into the third dimension as an elevation.

Students may cut out windows and doors and color, applique or furnish their rooms.

4-12   **SS • LA • A**

Foundation for Architecture, Philadelphia

104. MEASUREMENT FOR HUMAN PROPORTIONS

Introduce students to various ancient methods of measurement (Egyptian cubit, paces, outstretched arms, etc). Ask students to think of ways that they can use their own bodies to measure objects and distances. Point out that the width of one finger is useful for small distances, but that "paces" make more sense for the span of a room. Have the students make many **estimates** of measurements, and compare with a physical verification. Spend enough time on this activity that students can develop some degree of accuracy in their estimates. Students 4-12 can work in pairs. Compare these units of measurement to standard units (the width of two fingers is about an inch, etc.)

K-12   M • SS

Once students have considered different ways to use their own bodies as units of measure, have them consider the ways in which architectural proportions are geared to a human scale (doors must be tall and wide enough to walk through, a window must be set low enough that we can look through it, stairs must be geared to a human pace, a chair should be low enough that your feet can rest comfortably on the floor, etc.) Relate this idea to the story of "Goldilocks and the Three Bears". At home, students can look at a list of specific objects and architectural parts to see if they have been designed with proper attention to human scale. Young students in particular will notice that most of their home environment has been designed on an adult scale.

Have students measure specific items and decide, like Goldilocks, whether it is too high, too low, or just right (wide/narrow, big/little, etc.). Have an adult at home make the same decisions and compare the results.

Suggestions:
- the bathroom sink
- kitchen cabinets and counters
- your bed
- window sill
- shelves in your room
- door knob
- refrigerator handle
- stairs

K-12   M • SS

105. AVERAGING FOR HUMAN PROPORTIONS

The math skill of averaging takes on a clear meaning when applied to finding comfortable sizes for furniture. Have students take specific measurements from each other and average the answers to determine the most servicable dimensions for furniture, as well as heights for window sills, the pencil sharpener, shelves, etc.

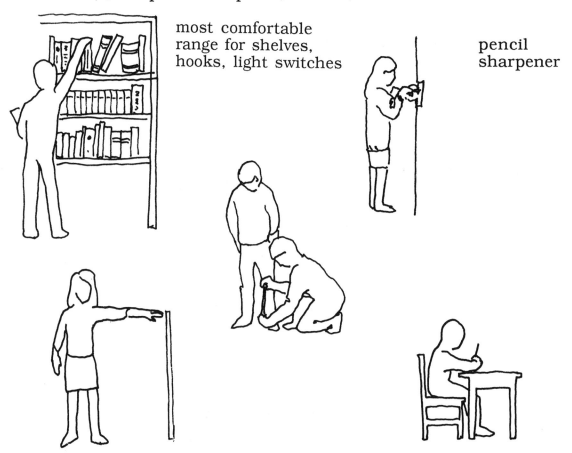

most comfortable range for shelves, hooks, light switches

pencil sharpener

The students are determining their own **scale**. Have them compare their findings with actual dimensions of class furniture and point out that the people who designed and manufactured the furniture used exactly the same criteria. Demonstrate how a giant or a tall adult would throw the measurements out of an appropriate scale.

5-12

S • M • SS • LA

106. ESTIMATING DISTANCES

Using both English and metric standards, have students make many estimates of specific objects (include girths) and dimensions in their classroom. Have them check their estimates with tape measures, rules, yardsticks, and meter sticks. Students should work in pairs, and be given several chances to estimate and verify so that they can shift from wild guesses to a realistic sense of distance. (Developing a sense of distance is an extremely valuable skill; estimation exercises can be repeated throughout the academic year, using the built environment as an ever-present reference point.)

3-12   **S • M**

107. PERIMETER, AREA AND VOLUME

Floor plans are an obvious source for students to determine perimeters, areas and volumes of particular spaces using the appropriate formulas. The volumes of skyscrapers can be generated through multiplication; the approximate volume of the school can be generated by teams of students taking measurements from different parts of the school and combining their results with those of the other teams. Students should make estimates on the results at various stages of their research; first estimates will be wild guesses which will become more and more realistic. (Complicated challenges require frequent conversion between inches and feet which may be prohibitively frustrating for students who are not confident with intricate arithmetic problems.)

4-12   **S • M**

108. SCALE AND RATIO

Students who have a firm grip on standard measuring skills can use scaled straightedges to project floor plans to an accurate scale. (Avoid calling the straightedge a "ruler", which has specific meaning to students.) Scale transformation is a sophisticated skill, and requires a great deal of guidance at first. Provide several easy examples, as provided in the following exercise.

Students can also use graph paper of various scales to project scaled down dimensions and to facilitate their drawings.

Students with the necessary math skills can determine the **ratio** of their scale drawing to its actual counterpart.

Scale 1"   = 1'   Ratio 1:12

Scale 1/2" = 1'   Ratio 1:24

Scale 1/4" = 1'   Ratio 1:48

Foundation for Architecture, Philadelphia

109. SCALED STRAIGHTEDGES

Students can use the following exercise as an introduction to scale transformation. (Do NOT refer to straightedges as rulers.) After some preliminary discussion, have students answer the questions. Expect initial confusion and reassure students that this skill will get easier with practice.

Once the students have grasped the concepts involved, have them back their straightedges with oak tag to use for their own scaled floor plans or for any activity involving scale transformations.

When backing the straightedges, use rubber cement to avoid buckling. Glue onto oak tag **first** and cut out **second**, to avoid misalignment.

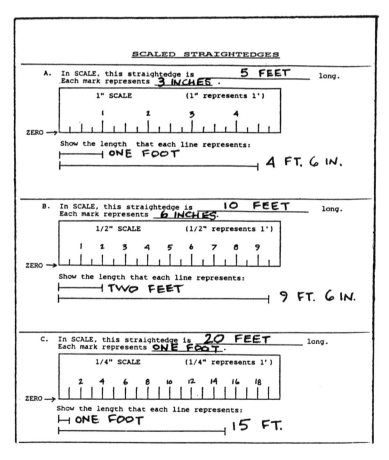

Introductory lesson with answers

Foundation for Architecture, Philadelphia

110. CAN YOU READ SCALED STRAIGHTEDGES?

A.　In SCALE, this straightedge is _____ long.
　　Each mark represents _____.

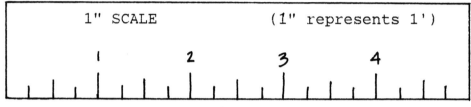

Show the length that each line represents:

B.　In SCALE, this straightedge is _____ long.
　　Each mark represents _____.

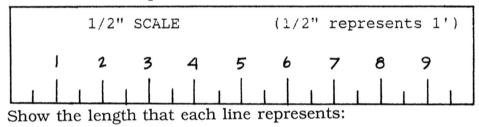

Show the length that each line represents:

C.　In SCALE, this straightedge is _____ long.
　　Each mark represents _____.

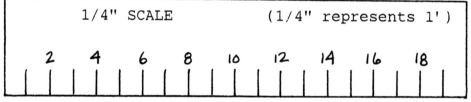

Show the length that each line represents:

Foundation for Architecture, Philadelphia

111. MAKE A FLOOR PLAN OF YOUR HOME

Students who are confident in their drafting and measuring abilities can attempt an extended floor plan of their homes. Do not underestimate the difficulty of this assignment; allow time for revisions and corrections. It is conceptually difficult for very young students to grasp the organization of passageways, halls, and stairways in two dimensions, and may take more than the first try for older students to get every room to "hook" up correctly with the others. Parents can be extremely helpful. Precise measurements would be too exacting for any but the most highly motivated students; this is a project in which estimating and retaining an approximate scale become valuable tools.

This project introduces students to the working method they will use later to make designs of their own.

If students have great difficulty in projecting rooms, have them take different colors of index cards to represent the different rooms. The cards have the advantage of being movable, so students can shift them around and cut them to fit. Once the cards are arranged correctly, students can glue them in place and add dimensions and symbols.

Graph paper is appropriate for a final product, or can be used under tracing paper, which is also an appropriate medium for finished work. Professional architects make use of both kinds of paper to help them maintain scale (as well as to keep their lines straight!); they also use sophisticated drafting tables that have special rulers and suspended pencils that enable them to control a drawing. Once your students have done some work on their own floor plans, take them to visit an architect's office so that they can see the "tools of the trade".

6-12   **S • M • A**

112. DESIGN AND CONSTRUCT YOUR DREAM ROOM

Have students take some time to brainstorm ideas for their Dream Room, using words, phrases, drawings and collage. They should first develop a journal of ideas and fantasies, much the way a working architect would, which will become the basis for a descriptive essay (i.e., the journal is an extended pre-writing exercise which enables students to organize their ideas into coherent written form).

The second stage of the activity is a floor plan; students should maintain a sense of scale, and can use scaled straightedges if appropriate to their skill level. Furniture should be included through simple symbols, also in correct scale.

The third stage is at least one elevation, or drawing of the room (with furniture) as it would appear in two dimensions. Students will now consider a color scheme.

The fourth stage is a model of the room, made either with a shoebox or a box made to different proportions out of stiff paper. Have students maintain scale by using a pipe-cleaner figure (see DESIGN).

This progression of activities (brainstorm/ write/ plan/ design/ construct) is useful for planning facades, buildings, and communities, depending on the amount of time allotted for the project. Students' imaginations will be stimulated through appropriate slides and a developing vocabulary which will encourage them to stretch their imaginations beyond conventional limits.

4-12   **M • SS • LA • A**

Foundation for Architecture, Philadelphia

113. ANALYZING PUBLIC INTERIORS

Using charts and floor plans, students will gather information to make a critical evaluation of a public space outside of school. Suggestions: a fast food restaurant, an office, the public library, a movie lobby, an arcade - any interior with comfortable public access.

Many issues are appropriate to a fully-developed research project, which can culminate in a design project in which each student will plan and construct a model of an improved version of this specialized place.

Issues to consider:

- the function of the space
- the five senses
- materials
- special architectural elements
- special equipment
- entrances and window use
- acoustics
- lighting (natural and artificial)
- color schemes
- energy systems
- furniture arrangement
- analysis of traffic and room use; safety exits; access for handicapped
- interviews of staff who use space

Both in their analysis of the existing space and in their ideas for improvement, students should always relate their remarks to whether or not the environment's **function** is effectively served; this is the criterion for judgement. Whether a student likes or dislikes a space is applicable only insofar as it can be related to the effectiveness of the elements. (As a parallel, a professional architect might not "like" a client's ideas or the final result of a project, but is often constrained by cost, pre-existing structures, public taste, lack of information, etc.)

6-12   **S • M • SS • LA • A**

114. VOCABULARY: INTERIORS

       access
       acoustics
       architectural elevation
       architectural plan, floor plan
       architectural section
       architectural elements (p. 96)
       atmosphere
       ambiance
       bubble diagram
       climate control
       energy systems (p. 93)
       function (purpose)
       furniture (p. 97)
       lighting
         - natural
         - artificial
         - incandescent
         - fluorescent
       materials (p. 52)
       measurement
         - perimeter
         - area
         - volume
         - average
         - ratio
         - scale
         - proportion
       passageway
       passive solar energy
       private
       public
       room (p. 96)
       social dynamics
       "traffic" patterns of people (circulation)

NOTE: The numbers following certain words refer to VOCABULARY LISTS which develop those topics in detail.

K-12
                                             S • M • SS • LA • A

Foundation for Architecture, Philadelphia

EXTERIORS

Students take a closer look at a variety of facade elements and their functions, and are given opportunities to make their own facade designs. Students are made aware of architectural clues to a building's function and its appropriate placement in a community, and use their accumulated knowledge for their own building designs.

EXTERIORS

115. DOORS AND WINDOWS: FOUR FUNCTIONS

Discuss with students the many aspects of doors and windows. Organize this information according to the following four functions.

1.   INVITATION: To welcome people and encourage them to go inside a building.

2.   PROTECTION: To keep certain people, animals and harsh weather out.

3.   DECORATION: To enhance a building's appearance and to make it unique.

4.   INFORMATION: To show where we live, to show business hours or display a product, etc.; to express a family or business through choice of design elements; to give a clue about what's inside.

The doors and windows of a structure should fulfill all of these functions in harmony with the purpose of the structure itself. (In a Gothic cathedral, the huge doorways flanked by statues of saints and the high stained glass windows express religious majesty and grandeur. A store might use an electric eye door to make it easy to exit with shopping bags, and uses large windows to display merchandise. A residential doorway has a house number and often a light to clarify the address and make the entrance visible at night. Many homeowners put seasonal displays on their front doors and in their windows.)

Show slides of a variety of different buildings and have students discuss the ways in which the doors and windows help to carry out the buildings' functions.

K-12   **S • SS • LA • A**

Foundation for Architecture, Philadelphia

116. VARIETIES OF DOORS AND WINDOWS

Show slides that cover a wide variety of door and window styles. Discuss the variations with reference to:

- four functions
- climate
- materials
- use
- styles and shapes

Door Varieties	Window Varieties
French	porthole
Dutch	rifle/arrow slit
garage	tracery
sliding	stained glass
glass	transom
steel	casement
portcullis/drawbridge	bay
hatch	double hung
trapdoor	blind
folding	fanlight
screen	picture
storm	display
revolving	frosted
electric eye	
arched	
swinging (saloon)	
porch	
louvered	

Take a neighborhood walk; have students draw or photograph a variety of door and window styles.

Handicap access

Discuss with students the importance of entrances for people in wheelchairs. Why are all **public** buildings supposed to have such an entrance? What features make an entrance easier for a person in a wheelchair (ramps, rails, wide doors that open easily). Does your school have an entrance like this? Can you find others?

K-12 **SS • LA**

Foundation for Architecture, Philadelphia

117. PAPER DOORS AND WINDOWS

Discuss with students the varieties of door and window styles. Have students cut shapes out of paper to make doors and windows that can swing open. Encourage students to be imaginative; brainstorm different shapes that might be used. Color or applique different materials.

EXAMPLES

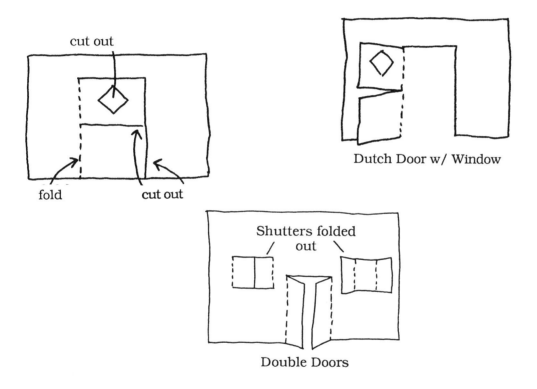

Dutch Door w/ Window

Double Doors

K-4   **SS • LA • A**

Paper can be bent, scored, folded, twisted, cut and slotted for very sophisticated projects.

4-6   **SS • LA • A**

118. SHOEBOX DOORS AND WINDOWS

Discuss aspects of doors and windows.

- function
- types
- materials

Show slides to demonstrate a wide variety of doors and windows:

- through time
- across cultures
- in different climates
- for different purposes

Each student will have a shoebox in which to design window and door shapes. Cut out the shapes; add glued materials for elaboration.

 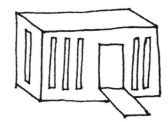 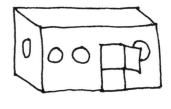

K-4   **SS • LA • A**

Older students should have a clear sense of the function of the "building" that they are designing and be able to relate their door and window choices to that function.

4-12   **SS • LA • A**

Foundation for Architecture, Philadelphia

119. ROOFS

Roofs can fulfill the same four functions as doors and windows. A roof can protect and decorate a building with its overhanging eaves and painted trim or cornice. Chimneys with smoke rising are a symbol of the cozy atmosphere inside, as well as an exterior indication of the building's interior construction. Curling ends at roof corners evoke the Orient; domes signal religious monuments; pointed domes are often Middle Eastern. Steeply pitched roofs imply a climate with heavy snowfalls; the flat roofs of the American south spread out beyond the walls to give shade. Cupolas and lanterns are roof top structures that give high vantage points for public information from bell-ringing or beacons; widow's walks originated as observation posts for women watching for their husbands to return from the sea or from the Civil War. Show slides of buildings and discuss with students the reasons for their shapes and designs.

Common roof varieties are shown in the ILLUSTRATED GLOSSARY.

K-12   **S • SS • LA**

Relate roofs to hats, which serve much the same purposes. Hats range from the functional to the decorative, depending on their purpose. Have students make hats that would be suitable for different climates. Start a class collection of hats and turn them into roofs; students will construct a building that the hat implies.

Chinese farmer hat

cowboy hat

baseball cap with visor

sun bonnet

sombrero

fur hat with earmuffs

K-12   **S • SS • LA • A**

Foundation for Architecture, Philadelphia

120. ILLUSTRATED FACADE GLOSSARY

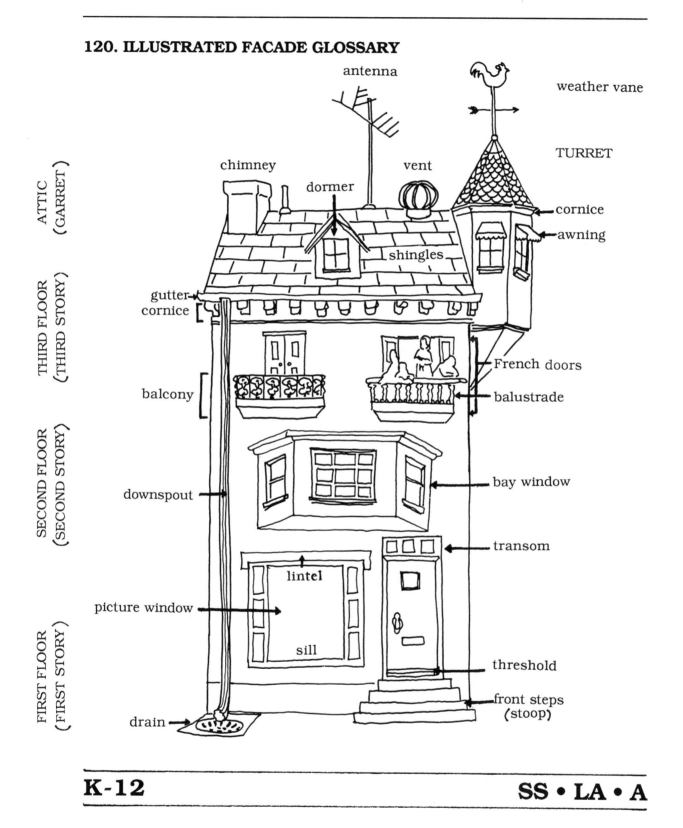

ATTIC (GARRET)

THIRD FLOOR (THIRD STORY)

SECOND FLOOR (SECOND STORY)

FIRST FLOOR (FIRST STORY)

antenna

weather vane

TURRET

chimney

dormer

vent

cornice

awning

shingles

gutter

cornice

French doors

balcony

balustrade

downspout

bay window

transom

lintel

picture window

sill

threshold

front steps (stoop)

drain

K-12

SS • LA • A

121. VOCABULARY: FACADE ELEMENTS

antenna
aluminum siding
arcade
arch
apartment
atrium
awning
busybody
building
balcony
balustrade
bannister
basement
bay
bay window
bracket
buttress
blind window
colonnade
casement window
chimney
clerestory
crenellation
column
cornice
corbel
cornerstone
capital
cupola
deck
display window
door
doorbell
door knob
door knocker
double-hung window
dome
downspout
dormer window
drain
edifice
eave
el
end

flashing
flying buttress
floor
foundation
fence
frieze
facade
fire escape
fan light
fenestration
fluorescent light
gate
garret
gutter
garage
gingerbread
gable
glazing
glass
- etched
- stained
- frosted
- leaded
house
house numbers
incandescent light
knocker
keyhole
keystone
latch
lantern
ledge
lattice
lintel
light
lightning rod
mailbox
moulding
mullion
mansard
newel
neon light
overhang

pier
pantile
porch
pane
peephole
portal
portico
pillar
pilaster
planter
picture window
pediment
quoin
railing
roof
rose window
sill
sign
spire
steeple
shutter
screen (door, window)
sash
skylight
storm window
step
stoop
structure
story
shingle
threshold
trim
transom
thatching
TV antenna
tower
turret
vent
verandah
weather vane
widow's walk
window
window box

K-12

S • SS • LA • A

Foundation for Architecture, Philadelphia

122. FACADE ELEMENTS: FUNCTION OR DECORATION?

Show slides of a variety of different facades. Focus on aspects taken from FACADE VOCABULARY. Have students point out elements in slides.

Discuss the reasons for various facade elements. Distinguish between **functional** and **decorative** aspects. With very sophisticated students, trace the historical development of certain elements which have lost their functional meaning in today's technology, such as quoins, pediments, etc. Analyze a specific facade together in these terms.

	Element	Functional Aspect	Decorative Aspect
1.	gutter	keeps rain off of roof, and off of sides of building	painted to go with trim color
2.	stained glass window	lets light in	colorful
3.	plain window	lets in light and air	windows make a pattern in facade; curtains look colorful
4.	stone and mortar	strong; hold up roof; keep house dry & warm	pattern; nice color of stone

4-12   **S • SS • LA**

123. SHOEBOX FACADES

For each student, make a plain facade shape out of oak tag or cardboard that will fit onto the bottom of a shoebox. Introduce students to basic facade elements and vocabulary. Each student will draw the outlines of doors and windows on the paper.   Cut out the window shapes. Cut the doors so that they are "hinged". Using various scrap materials, crayons, and paint, the students will color and applique their facades. Chimneys, awnings, shutters, roofs and steps may be added by folding and gluing paper. Glue these facades onto the shoeboxes.

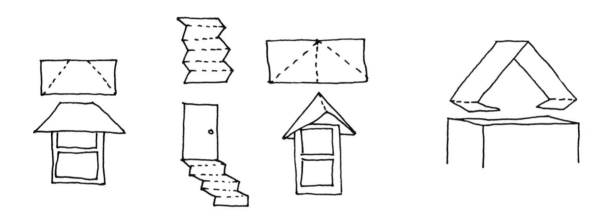

The "houses" can be assembled as a continuous row, or the other sides can be similarly covered so that the houses can stand separately in a neighborhood arrangement.

K-4   **SS • LA • A**

Foundation for Architecture, Philadelphia

124. DESK FACADES

Introduce the students to a basic vocabulary of facade elements. On stiff paper or on cardboard large enough to fit the front of the students' desks, the students will draw facades with reference to their vocabulary words. Have the students add color, texture, and applique to their facades (yarn, sand paper, awnings, tin foil, window sashes, etc.) Students will tape their completed facades to the fronts of their desks to make streetscapes.

K-4 **SS • LA • A**

Foundation for Architecture, Philadelphia

125. CLAY FACADES AND SHADOW PATTERNS

Older students can take advantage of the dimensional possibilities of clay to make a highly articulated facade (as in bas-relief) which can then be lit from different angles to produce different shadows. (Renaissance and Baroque architects were sensitive to the way light played over the forms of their facades at different times of day. Often, such landmark buildings have become tourist attractions and are floodlit from below at night, producing some startling new effects.)

In conjunction with this project, students should find a highly articulated facade pattern in a local building and make two drawings at opposite ends of the day, to maximize the difference in the pattern of the shadows. (The location of the sun and time of day should be indicated.)

8-12   **A • SS • LA**

Foundation for Architecture, Philadelphia

126. BUILDING TYPES

With the students, generate a list of the different kind of buildings that make up a town. (Vocabulary list follows.)

Cut out a variety of different facade shapes from this list. Keep a consistent scale.

Hold up a facade and let the students guess what kind of building it could be. The student who makes the most appropriate guess receives that facade to decorate. (Very young children might not recognize many of the traditional "types". In that case, they may make any suggestion to "win" the facade and may decorate it as they please.)

SUGGESTED PATTERNS:

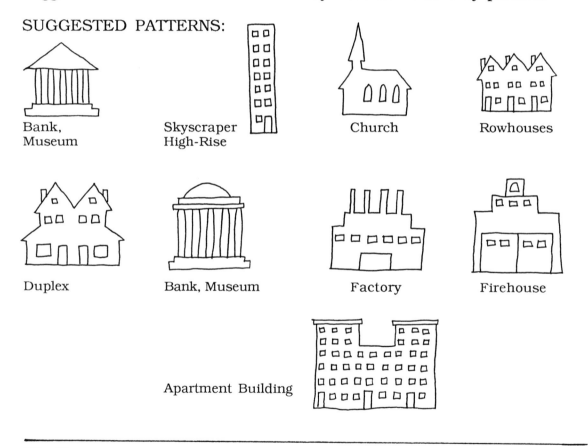

Bank, Museum

Skyscraper High-Rise

Church

Rowhouses

Duplex

Bank, Museum

Factory

Firehouse

Apartment Building

K-6

SS • LA • A

127. VOCABULARY: BUILDING TYPES

aqueduct
adobe pueblo
arcade
amusement park
apartment building
animal homes
 - nest
 - den
 - lair
 - dam
 - web
 - hole
 - eaves
 - chimney
art gallery
auto body shop
airport
bridge
 - suspension
 - foot
 - log
 - cantilever
 - truss
bank
bakery
barn
church
cottage
clothing store
city hall
campus
college
canal, lock
cooling towers
castle
cupola
construction site
carport
cave
circus tent
cemetery
carriage house
doctor's office
dam
duplex
dog house
dance studio
doll house

department store
dwelling
diner
edifice
fire house
fountain
farm
factory
fast food building
facade
government building
garden apartment
ghetto
gas station
greenhouse
gazebo
garage
grocery store
hogan
hospital
haunted house
house
hangar
"house of cards"
hotel
home
hut
igloo
library
lean to
lighthouse
laboratory
log cabin
mansion
mosque
monument
memorial
mall
museum
motel
movie house
mobile home
nuclear generator
observatory
office building
pagoda
pizza shop
portico

post office
pier, dock
park
pyramid
prison
penthouse
projects
power house (generator)
police station
professional building
radio station
reservoir
rowhouse
ranch house
recreational buildings
race track
residence
synagogue
supermarket
skyscraper
store
storefront
school
stable
slum
skating rink
stadium
stage settings
silo
shack
temple
tower
teepee
train station
trailer
trailer park
trinity
twin
tree house
tool shed
tent
tenement
university
windmill
warehouse
yurt
ziggurat
zoo

K-12   **S • SS • LA • A**

128. CLUES TO BUILDING TYPES

Show slides of a variety of building types. Use obvious examples, and avoid signage so that students must depend on architectural clues. Students will guess what the building is used for, and tell what clues the building gives them (i.e. a large display window indicates a store; Greek columns and a large stairway indicate a bank or museum; a large steel door indicates a garage or warehouse; a window box with flowers indicates a residence). Keep a list of the architectural elements noted by the students; ask leading questions to guide them (what might go in and out of this door? Why does this [apartment] building have so many windows.) Stress the function of the building.

K-12 **SS • LA**

Show slides of architectural **details** which are clues to a building's type (Greek capital, porthole, barn door, flying buttress, stained glass window). Once the students have correctly identified the building type, add these clues to the previous list.

4-12 **SS • LA**

For research, have students check the etymologies of the words we use for building types, and find their historical referents. (A *stadium* is a Greek word, based on a measure of length used for the course of a footrace, which was surrounded with tiers of seats. A *coliseum* is based on the Roman *Colosseum*; similar backgrounds can be found for *arcade, museum, ghetto, synagogue, reservoir, aqueduct*, etc.) This research can help students understand the meaning of an architectural cliche and the reasons so many architects try to invent new forms (usually against popular opinion!)

6-12 **SS • LA • A**

129. CLUES TO THE CLASSIFICATION OF BUILDING TYPES

It is important that students come to make generalizations about types of buildings in order to make decisions in later work about **zoning** and **city planning**. A factory is different from a warehouse in function, but they are both industrial buildings and would be classified together. Show slides of buildings from the different classifications and have students look for common architectural elements.

Classification	Example	Clues
1. Residential	homes	front yard, small windows, chimney, person-sized door
	apartment building	lots of windows, curtains and lamps in windows, many doors
2. Commercial	stores	display window, signs, picture of product
3. Industrial	factory, warehouse	large buildings with large doors, small or closed-up windows
4. Institutional	hospital, school	large building, many different entrances, plain design
5. Monumental	memorials, museums	fancy architecture, large, easy to see from a distance, statue on top, landscaping, located away from other buildings
6. Recreational	skating rink, stadium, arcade	big parking lot, easy access for public, informal architecture

Foundation for Architecture, Philadelphia

130. SKYLINE MURAL

Define a skyline as the **silhouette** that buildings make against the sky.

Prepare a long skyline on a length of brown butcher or craft paper. Students will complete the facade implied by the skyline, filling in doors, windows, architectural elements, color, pattern and texture.

This mural can provide the backdrop for a variety of other projects, especially facade projects which will be oriented towards a frontal view. Students may add "street furniture" (signs, poles, bus stops, etc.)

K-8   **SS • LA • A**

Foundation for Architecture, Philadelphia

131. BUILDING TYPES: CLIMATE AND GEOGRAPHY

Show slides of buildings that reflect changing needs in different natural environments. Include "primitive" dwellings, which are made from immediately available natural products.

Discuss:

How do building **styles** change in different climates or terrains?

- hot areas: tents, thickly-walled buildings, open windows, awnings, verandahs
- high rainfall: houses on stilts, solid foundations, gutters, downspouts
- mountains: steeply-sloped roofs for snow to slide off
- extremely cold areas: igloos, homes centered around a fireplace, small doorways and windows
- wind: windmills, low buildings, windbreaks

What building **materials** become available in different areas?

- Arctic: ice for igloos
- forest: wood
- rain forest: vines, large leaves, plant fibers, tree trunks
- desert: mud for adobe bricks

K-12   **S • SS • LA • A**

Foundation for Architecture, Philadelphia

132. WHAT KIND OF HOME WOULD YOU NEED?

Develop a variety of distinct natural environments to describe to your students; have them choose one of the environments and imagine a suitable dwelling.

Suggested environments and climates:

- jungle or rain forest (wild animals, hot, lots of rain, lots of trees, vines and big leaves, rivers)
- desert (hot and dry, sometimes windy, sandy, cactus plants, small animals)
- outer space (robots, spaceships, pressure suits, cold, no atmosphere, no gravity, advanced technology)
- Arctic (very cold, snow and ice, seals, walrus, penguins, little color in landscape)
- city (tall buildings, lots of traffic, subways, seasonal changes)
- island (forests, rivers, cliffs, waterfalls, surrounded by ocean, hot, danger of storms and tidal waves).

When the students are imagining their dwellings, they should consider specific issues:

- What would your home be made out of?
- What would be around your home? (Plants, terrain, other buildings)
- Would anyone else live near you?
- What would your front door be like?
- What kind of windows would you have?
- What rooms would you have?
- Where would you sleep? What kind of bed would you make?
- Where would you make your food?

Students will draw a picture and develop a diorama that describes this home in its natural context. Students should be able to explain their design choices in terms of the environment (context).

K-12

S • SS • LA • A

Foundation for Architecture, Philadelphia

133. BUILDING TYPES ACROSS CULTURES

Societies express themselves graphically through their architecture. The raw materials provided by the land, the climatic needs, and the cultural priorities are combined into a distinct, and unique, three-dimensional form. Any particular civilization can be investigated through its buildings and their arrangements.

In discussion using slides or photo essays, or in research papers, students should address several issues:

- climate and geography
- level of technologic sophistication of the culture
- the functions of the building types as they reflect social mores. (Greek amphitheaters and auditoriums were designed for democratic forums as well as for dramatic presentations, both being distinctive aspects of their society. Stonehenge and many other prehistoric monuments show a culture's attention towards astronomical events, which were important for religious and agricultural reasons. Roman baths played an important social and recreational role, and also reflect Roman architectural sophistication in terms of underground heating and drainage systems, etc.)
- the placement and relative sizes of the buildings in relation to their types and functions. (A medieval cathedral was centrally placed and scaled so large that it dwarfed the rest of the town. Kin relationships are often expressed by the relative proximity of residences in a tribal village, etc.)

See BIBLIOGRAPHY for books on specific cultures.

K-12   **SS • LA • A**

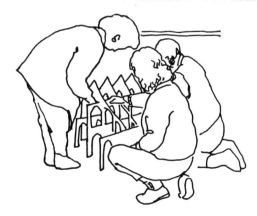

Foundation for Architecture, Philadelphia

134. BUILDING TYPES THROUGH HISTORY

As with Activity #133, architecture expresses the development through time of changes in technological possibilities as well as the shifting of empires and trade relations. Architectural styles mix as cultures do, presenting hybrid or totally new forms. Students should be able to recognize architectural styles from several historical epochs. Use slides and photo essays, and have students make their own drawings of historic landmarks of architecture in which they label distinctive stylistic devices and explain their functions. It would be impossible to make an exhaustive list of buildings suitable for study as there are so many. A few obvious examples would include:

Prehistoric: Stonehenge
Sumeria: ziggurat, cities, irrigation systems
Egypt: pyramids, cliff tombs, temples, cities
Mycenae: Treasury of Atreus (Agamemnon's Tomb)
Greece: Parthenon, Acropolis, amphitheaters, cities
Rome: aqueducts, viaducts, baths, Pantheon, Colosseum, Forum,
       Pompeii, Hadrian's Wall, roads
The Seven Wonders of the Ancient World: The Great Pyramid at Giza,
       The Temple at Ephesus, The Hanging Gardens of Babylon,
       The Statue at Olympia, The Mausoleum at Halicarnassus, The
       Colossus of Rhodes, The Pharos (Lighthouse) at Alexandria
China: Buddhist temples, gardens, homes, Great Wall
Japan: pagodas, temples, gardens, homes
Islam: Hagia Sophia, mosques, minarets
India: Taj Mahal, rock-cut temples
Thailand: Angkor Wat
Pre-Columbian: Aztec, Maya, Inca; Macchu Picchu
Medieval Europe: castles, cathedrals, hill towns, walled towns
Renaissance Europe: St. Peter's Cathedral, Leaning Tower of Pisa
Modern Europe: Bauhaus styles, Eiffel Tower
Early U.S.: native American dwellings: pioneer homes, Colonial
       architecture
Contemporary U.S.: Empire State Building, World Trade Towers,
       Astrodome, St. Louis Arch, Capitol Building, motels, diners

See BIBLIOGRAPHY for historical reference books.

4-12   **SS • LA • A**

135. BUILDING TYPES: RELIGIOUS

Show slides of monuments of the most widespread religions of the world; Christianity, Judaism, Buddhism, and Islam. Have students make note of the architectural clues that distinguish church (cathedral), synagogue, temple, and mosque.

4-12   **SS • LA**

Show slides of the city of Jerusalem. Explain that it is a city of three religions: Judaism, Christianity and Islam. Focus on images of temples, mosques and churches. Discuss the architectural symbols used by each religion as well as the features common to all of the buildings (public spaces designed according to religious orientation of people inside, decoration reflecting religious orientation).

Discuss the importance of each group being able to express its belief through architecture, dress and customs.

Older students may want to discuss the tensions caused by cultural conflicts and study the current problems faced by disparate religious groups. They can use the newspaper to find articles about the cultures reflected by these architectural types.

6-12   **SS • LA**

Show slides of each type in the United States to remind students of the importance of religious tolerance in the founding of our country.

4-12   **SS • LA**

136. DESIGN YOUR "DREAM BUILDING"

Once the students have developed a vocabulary, become aware of the functions and varieties of materials, and learned to use architectural planning techniques, they may start an extended project based on their own fantasies.

Ask students to think about a dream building which they will design according to these systems. Each student should develop an essay to describe the building's purpose. Include function, location, materials, the number of rooms, the use of the rooms, and furniture.

Students can develop their plans through the following stages:

1. statement of function (purpose) of the building

2. journal of ideas(written, drawn, or collage)

3. descriptive essay

4. matrices of room use and relationships

5. bubble diagrams

6. floor plans

7. section and elevation

8. projection of materials

9. construction of a model

This project can be as elaborate as time permits. A rich background in architectural possibilities and effects will provide an expansive reference for the students' expression.

4-12   **M • SS • LA • A**

Foundation for Architecture, Philadelphia

137. THE ARCHITECT AND THE CLIENT

Architects seldom get to make their own "dream buildings". In almost every case, the architect is trying to make a design that fits another person's needs. This person, called the client, hires the architect and gives a list of requirements which the architect must satisfy in the design. Some clients are very single-minded; others are willing to let the architect play a large role in designing the project. Have your students role play this situation by dividing them into architect/client pairs; the clients will develop a "needs list" and the architect will design a building in the hopes of satisfying these needs. After an initial briefing, let the architects and clients both take some time to draw a quick floor plan and/or elevation based on these ideas. Compare the architects' and clients' drawings! The second session should be an effort for the architects to incorporate both sets of ideas. Remind students that the client has the ultimate say in the matter. This exercise is not only a chance for negotiation between students, but also an insight into the difficulties an architect must face in professional life.

K-6 | **SS • LA • A**

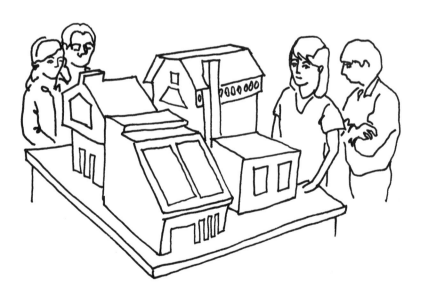

Foundation for Architecture, Philadelphia

138. ZOOS

Contemporary zoo design has shifted far away from being a series of cages, and offers many interesting challenges for students. In discussion, it is important to stress that a zoo must enclose the animals for two reasons:

1. the safety of the public

2. the safety and comfort of the animal

The second point is often not as obvious as the first. Animals have unique and disparate needs as they are often taken from specialized ecosystems. Their environments must have adequate climate control, enough room and familiar terrain, and often exotic food. Equally important, the animal must be protected from the public. For reasons ranging from friendly ignorance to malice, some people will throw the animals food that disrupts or harms their diets, or will throw objects, yell or whistle at the animals to animate them. Students can gain insight into the responsibilities of proper care and respectful attendance of zoo animals.

After a discussion of these basic principles of zoo-keeping, have students choose an animal to research. Through floor plans, contour maps, elevations, and sections, the students will design an enclosure for the animal and should be able to give appropriate explanations for choices of

- scale
- materials
- terrain
- shelter from weather
- climate control
- sleeping quarters
- feeding

Before students put their design plans into three dimensional form, each should model the animal itself (out of clay or other material) in order to establish the appropriate scale. (If the dioramas are to be assembled later, the model animals should be in approximate scale to each other, although liberties must be taken if the range is between an elephant and a lizard.)

When each model is completed, students may assemble them into a zoo. This kind of project is akin to CITY PLANNING and will require democratic discussion and negotiation in the class. Issues to consider include:

- arrangement (Which animals seem to "go together"? Which animals have comparable needs, as pools of water, dense foliage, or rocky terrain? Would it be practical to group the animals according to their habitats?)
- public access and movement (pathways and parking, entrances)
- public comfort: benches, shelters, rest rooms, refreshments, parking
- financial support: admission gate, gift shop

A field trip to your local zoo will be most useful **after** the students have started their own designs, as they will be more able to focus on the decisions made by the zoo's designers. Members of the zoo's staff will be delighted to discuss their own challenges and solutions with knowledgeable students, and will be able to give students insight into the truly complex needs of many of the animals.

K-12   S • LA • A

139. VOCABULARY: ZOOS

ecosystem
environment
habitat
terrain
ecology
preservation
conservation
endangered species

4-12   S • LA

140. ARCHITECTURE IN ADVERTISING

Look through magazines to see how architectural elements are used to express qualities about a product.

EXAMPLES:

- an ornate facade as the backdrop for an expensive car (express luxury)
- a swimming pool as a backdrop for a menthol cigarette (express coolness, refreshment)
- a shiny kitchen as a backdrop for a cleanser
- a suburban house as a backdrop for a life insurance company (express security, affluence).

6-12   **SS • LA**

141. REAL ESTATE ADS

Have students check the newspaper for real estate ads. Decipher the abbreviations with them and develop a list. Students can discuss why those particular features are mentioned.

Have students write imaginative real estate ads for their own designs. If they were to write an ad for a culture that did not have newspapers (as, for a castle), explain that this in an **anachronism**.

Students should make note of the catchy titles or words often used to describe buildings in these ads: Quaint, Quiet, Secluded, Home on the Range, etc. Point out that these phrases are often **euphemisms**; a "Handyman Special" usually refers to a shambles, and "Secluded" might mean isolated or difficult to get to. Why would real estate companies use euphemisms to describe the properties that they are trying to sell? Have students make up some euphemisms of their own to gloss over a building's defects.

4-12   **SS • LA**

NEIGHBORHOODS AND STREETS

With an emphasis on neighborhood walks, students use drawings, maps and photography to study a living community as an integral series of interwoven systems with a direct impact on the residents.

NEIGHBORHOODS AND STREETS

142. WHAT IS A NEIGHBORHOOD?

Webster's Dictionary relates a neighborhood to the Anglo-Saxon word *neahgebur*, or "nigh-dweller". Thus a neighborhood is defined by a sense of "closeness". Closeness has two meanings: the **denotation** is of physical proximity and the **connotation** is of personal bonds or friendliness. Thus, a neighborhood has both physical and psychological boundaries.

Ask students how they would define a neighborhood and elicit these two points in discussion. Have students brainstorm a list that defines the school's neighborhood, including not only specific buildings and streets, but also features of landscape and terrain, natural boundaries, and **qualities** of the neighborhood. Use this group discussion as an introduction for students to write a description and definition of their own neighborhoods. Ensuing activities will enlarge and clarify their insights.

4-12   **SS • LA**

143. MENTAL MAPS: WHERE IS YOUR NEIGHBORHOOD?

Have students develop a **mental** map of their own neighborhoods, to be made without any references. These maps will be distorted and incomplete, which is exactly their importance. Encourage students to skip the parts that they can't remember, as these maps have the value of showing the students' **personal** associations with their neighborhoods. It is also a good way to start developing the students' powers of observation. Keep these first maps intact, but have students make second maps with corrections and additions, or develop **cumulative** maps.

4-12   **M • SS • A**

144. CUMULATIVE MAPS

After students have made mental maps, they will make a second map of the same area, using official maps for reference. This map will be cumulative, in that, once the streets and natural boundaries are defined, students will begin to fill in buildings, parks, and other landmarks as they become more conscious of them through neighborhood walks and other research techniques generated in class. These maps should be drawn on paper large enough for students to be able to add whatever labels, symbols, explanations, and colors they need, and should be developed in stages. The final result can be displayed with the original mental maps; their comparison will show students the difference between their **subjective** perception and **objective** information.

4-12   **M • SS • LA • A**

As a class project, students can pool information for a large cumulative map of the school neighborhood. Begin with individual mental maps, which will show that each student has a unique subjective perception of the area. Students can work in teams to research different aspects over several weeks.

4-12   **M • SS • LA • A**

145. MAP YOUR ROUTE TO SCHOOL

Have students develop maps to show their routes to school. Again, compare mental and cumulative maps. Students can use street maps and the maps published by public transportation companies for reference, which can be marked with a highlighter marker for initial research. Students should make note of personal highlights of the route as well as of natural and built landmarks.

4-12   **M • SS • LA • A**

146. DESCRIBE YOUR ROUTE TO SCHOOL

Once students have completed maps of their routes, they will write **directions** explaining how to get from their home to school. This activity might be in letter form, written to an imaginary or real person who knows nothing about the area and needs **explicit** directions. Students should refer to compass points, specific numbers of blocks, street names, public transportation routes (i.e. "the #9 bus, the A Train, etc.), and landmarks ("turn left at the gas station, go to the next traffic light," etc.) Students should read each other's descriptions and edit for vague or confusing directions to help in revisions. Students will come to see that often a **combination** of words and pictures is the most useful method for describing a route.

4-12   **SS • LA**

147. MAP PUZZLES

Introductory map activities can use maps as puzzles; such use is also helpful for students with undeveloped drawing skills. Make or enlarge a map of a familiar area and cut it into **jigsaw** pieces for students to assemble, using street names as guides. Draw an enlarged map of a familiar area and leave out all street names for students to fill in, using a neighborhood walk to fill in unknown streets. Use "**blank maps**" for students to fill in with buildings, building types, landscapes and natural boundaries, parks, etc. as in a scavenger hunt.

4-12   **M • SS • LA**

Foundation for Architecture, Philadelphia

148. COLOR CODES FOR BUILDING TYPES

Introduce students to color coding by distinguishing the classifications of building types on an enlarged map of the school neighborhood. For example, **residential** buildings (homes) would be blue, **industrial** buildings gray, **recreational** buildings green, and so on, to include **commercial, monumental** and **institutional** buildings as well.

Color coding will enable students to see how buildings tend to be grouped (a religious building in the midst of homes, groups of stores separate from groups of homes, etc.). This activity is a good introduction to zoning.

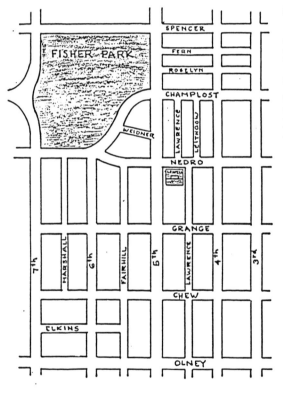

COLORS: CLASSIFICATIONS

BLUE: residential
YELLOW: commercial
GRAY: industrial
GREEN: recreational
RED: monumental
PURPLE: institutional

LOWELL SCHOOL NEIGHBORHOOD
COLOR THE MAP WITH THE COLORS SHOWN ABOVE

Foundation for Architecture, Philadelphia

149. MAP SYMBOLS

Have students use symbols such as these to describe a neighborhood. Students can invent symbols, which should always be explained on the map in a **legend**.

- compass, or arrow showing North
- buildings
- train tracks
- synagogue
- church
- mosque
- school
- library
- hospital

- gas station
- high rise or skyscraper
- restaurant
- trees
- water
- streets
- parking lot
- bus stop
- subway, trolly, train

Foundation for Architecture, Philadelphia

150. ARCHITECTURAL SCAVENGER HUNTS

Using maps, pictures, words, or a combination, have students look for specific architectural elements and landmarks in the school neighborhood.

K-12   **SS • LA**

Split the students into teams. Each group will take the same route through the neighborhood but in opposite directions. Each team has a list of architectural elements clearly visible along the route. The team must find the element and record its location (street address). The elements may or may not be in order, depending on the independence and acuity of the students and the safety of the neighborhood streets.

6-12   **SS • LA**

Students may also use the images as directions for their walk, as, "Proceed to the blue arched doorway". At each location, the students will photograph the element. These pictures will be developed and used to label a neighborhood map.

6-12   **SS • LA**

Following are a few examples of pictures to use for scavenger hunts:

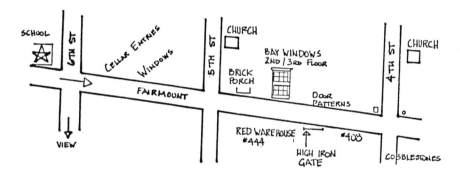

Use a **map** for a scavenger hunt. Students will circle items as they find them.

4-12   **M • SS • LA**

Use **visual checklists** for scavenger hunts.

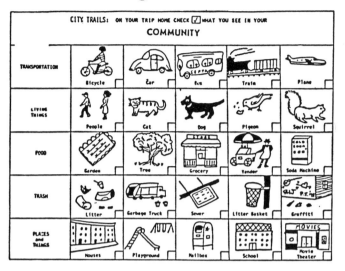

K-3 **SS • LA**

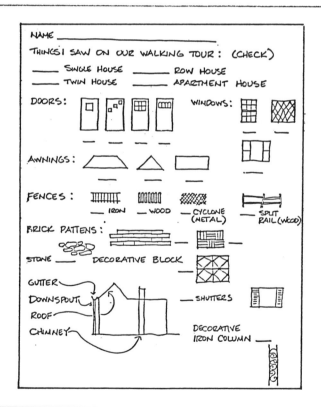

4-12 **SS • LA**

Foundation for Architecture, Philadelphia

151. NEIGHBORHOOD WALKS

Take at least one class walk through a neighborhood to give your class a first-hand look at the many issues that they have studied. Always have a specific focus established before you go. Neighborhood walks can be repeated around different topics, and are the best ways for students to research cumulative maps.

Sample questions for student discussion:

Why are there fences around gardens?
Why are there metal bars over basement windows?
Why are some porches enclosed and others open?
Why do stores have large windows along the street?
What does an air conditioner do?
Why are storm doors and windows used?
Why are there lintels over windows and doors?
What is the purpose of shutters on the sides of a window?
What is the purpose of an awning over a window?

Questions can tie into any aspect of your curriculum, and may be increasingly sophisticated.

K-12   **SS • LA**

Have students develop their own **visual glossaries** of architectural elements on a neighborhood walk. Students may use cameras or drawing skills to find and record examples from vocabulary lists, which will be labelled back in class for notebooks or class display.

4-12   **SS • LA • A**

Have students look for **cornerstones** or **plaques** on buildings, bridges, statues and other structures that will give them information about the **dates** the structures were made. Plaques often mention other facts about the structure, such as artists or designers, dimensions, commemorative information, or presiding government officials.

6-12   **SS**

Have each student pick a favorite color. Take a neighborhood walk and have each student find everything that is that color en route. Students with adequate writing skills should make a list of the architectural elements that they find and draw one example.

K-6   LA • A

Let your students test their powers of **memory** by selecting one building to take mental notes about. They must retain enough information to draw the building back in the classroom. The point of this activity is **not** to emphasize the students' poor memories but to find out which aspects of a building are retained, exaggerated or never noticed. Relate these distortions to mental maps, which show **subjective** perceptions. Stress the importance of these perceptions and encourage students to make incomplete drawings from memory so that they will become aware of the design's **impact** on their perceptions. Students may make a second or "corrected" drawing back on site, which will be an **objective** image.

Have several students work from the same building and compare their subjective drawings, to show that a building's design will have a different impact on different people. Note which elements are retained by most students.

4-12   SS • A

Develop your students' powers of observation by having them make a drawing in class of a building chosen from a neighborhood walk. Students may not use any sketches, words or photographs to help them. When they need more information, they must go back to the building and observe it. This exercise will force students to look at the building in different ways. Guide them through a list of specific information that must be included in the drawing; correct number, placement, pattern and relative size of windows; placement and decoration of doorways; roof structure; cornice design; scale of building in relation to adjacent buildings; materials; etc.

8-12   SS • A

Foundation for Architecture, Philadelphia

Students should observe the position of the **sun** and the direction of **shadows** cast by buildings, poles, etc. as they relate to **compass points**. Students should be able to point to the directions where the sun rises and sets, and observe that in northern latitudes, there is often one face of each building that never receives direct sunlight. (This, the north face, is the one preferred by artists, who often speak of "northern exposure". Artists want their studio windows to face north because they want diffused, even light for their work rather than the harsh glare and shadows that come from a southern exposure.)

See if students can think of "what lies beyond" their immediate view of the neighborhood in each direction. If they have been studying from maps of your town and city, they should be able to imagine that City Hall is to the west, the Memorial Tower is north, etc. See how far students can stretch their boundaries. (In which direction is California? Canada? South America? The Arctic?)

4-12   **S • SS**

Have students make note of the changing **skyline** as they walk through a neighborhood. These changes are due to the shifts in the students' **perspective**. Have each student pick a convenient spot and make four skyline drawings, one for each cardinal point (north, east, south, west) of the compass.

6-12   **SS • LA • A**

Foundation for Architecture, Philadelphia

152. MEET YOUR NEIGHBORS

Give your students an opportunity to learn about their neighborhoods from the **residents**. Make up a questionnaire for students to use in interviews. Questions may focus on a variety of topics:

- different interpretations of the neighborhood; perceived boundaries, landmarks, and qualities; which aspects are agreed upon; which aspects are the least defined

- history of the neighborhood; reasons for living there; changes in local buildings and businesses; changes in transportation systems; memories of and wishes for the neighborhood

- gardens, lawns and landscaping projects of neighbors; time and planning involved; names of plants; favorite or most successful aspects; growing techniques

- energy systems of houses; "side effects" of different fuels and systems; efficiency; residents' weatherizing projects

- local business owners and vendors; stories of setting up business in the area; who uses the business; how businesses have changed in the area

- negative aspects of the neighborhood; desired changes; ideas for implementing changes; potential political figures to address for help

4-12   **SS • LA**

Such research can easily generate class projects for helping a neighborhood, such as litter clean up, a visit to a convalescent home, a graffiti paint-over, etc.

4-12   **SS**

Foundation for Architecture, Philadelphia

153. LANDSCAPING

Show slides of a variety of different aspects of landscape architecture. Explain that most of the plants and land formations close to buildings have usually been at least partly modified; most sites in urban areas were originally forested, so it can usually be assumed that trees were cleared, perhaps a few hundred years ago. On a neighborhood walk watch for:

- plantings (trees in a row, hedges, gardens, wind breaks)
- clearings
- natural areas unchanged by the built environment
- embankments, canals, or leveled areas where the original form of the earth has been changed for sidewalks, streets, and building foundations

Discuss the reasons for landscaping designs:

- aesthetics (color and texture of gardens and trees)
- energy (trees block the wind and offer shade)
- privacy
- ecology (healthy areas have many plant, bird and animal species; which are indications of healthy air and water for people, too)

Discuss the difficulties encountered in landscape maintenance:

- tree roots close to buildings can crack foundations
- dead trees or branches (a blighted tree can spread disease to other trees, dead limbs might fall and hurt property)
- tree branches or vines on utility wires or blocking street lights
- hidden entrances or views blocked for drivers and pedestrians
- invasive plants
- maintenance (mowing lawns, weeding gardens, pruning hedges, watering plants)
- insect control; mole damage
- leash and curbing regulations for dogs (harmful effects of urine, feces and digging holes)

Students should learn to recognize a few of the most prevalent shade trees indigenous to their area. Students may come up with a landscaping project for their school or raise money to buy and plant a tree.

K-12   **SS • LA**

154. PARKS AND PLAYGROUNDS

Discuss with students the need for recreational areas in a neighborhood, as in parks and public playgrounds.

- What activities take place? (bike riding, roller skating, walking, walking dogs, sitting and talking, reading, playing chess or checkers, picnics)
- What elements are built into these environments to facilitate and encourage these activities? (open space, grass, trees, and plants, benches, walkways, playing equipment, statues, fountains)
- Who are the parks for? (Although parks are "public" areas, it is usually assumed that they will serve the needs of local residents; the size of this audience will affect the park's size.)
- What are the rules in parks and playgrounds? (no littering, don't hurt the grass or plants, play fair, clean up after your dog) Why do we need these rules? What does "No Loitering" mean?

K-12   S • LA

Have students find local parks and playgrounds on a city map. How are they designated? Mark them with a highlighter and discuss their relative locations. Do all neighborhoods have access to a park? Are all of the parks the same size? Is there an area that needs more parks?

4-12   M • SS

Have students visit a local park and evaluate it, using criteria similar to that in Activity #113. Working from these evaluations, students can re-design or create a new park. Students should be able to give appropriate reasons for their design choices.

4-12   SS • LA • A

Foundation for Architecture, Philadelphia

155. STREETSCAPES

As a parallel to a landscape, a **streetscape** is the sum total of external elements of the built environment; **"street furniture"** consists of facades, utility poles, telephone poles, wires, hydrants, lights, meters, vents, ducts, sewer gates, cables, man-hole covers, traffic signs, traffic lights, etc. These objects are not arbitrarily placed; students should learn to see them as the outward, visible indications of a vast network of energy and safety systems interwoven through the neighborhood and its environs. David Macaulay's book *Underground* has remarkably clear illustrations of the underground sources and connections of these systems.

K-12   **S • SS • LA**

There are many ways for students to categorize street furniture:

- **systems**: energy, communication, transportation, health, safety
- **utilities**: water, gas, electricity, phone
- **public vs. private use**: (a main water pipe would be considered public, but pipes going into a home would be private)

4-12   **S • SS • LA**

Students can work together to develop a mural of a local streetscape, with labels for street furniture and indications of above- and below-ground connections.

4-12   **S • SS • LA**

Students can take a look at their own homes and draw pictures to show how their homes connect to public systems.

4-12   **S • SS • LA**

156. STREET SMARTS

As students come to focus on aspects of streetscapes they should articulate the necessity for safety rules. Study the etymology of *pedestrian* and have students distinguish between foot traffic and automobile traffic. What kinds of traffic signals can students find on a local street? (A PED XING sign is for cars; cross-walks at inter-sections are for pedestrians; a traffic light is for both, etc.)

K-12   **SS • LA**

Students can develop a bulletin board of **traffic signs**, which should be labelled with their meanings. Students should make note of the combinations of **words** and **symbols** in road signs, as well as the **shapes** and **colors** used (the red octagon STOP sign is an example of long tradition; because of its special shape, a STOP sign can be recognized even from the back.) The standard arrangements of traffic lights (red on top, etc.) makes them readable for color-blind people. Many new symbols are now coming into use based on an **international** code so that people can understand traffic signs in other countries.

K-12   **SS • LA • A**

Students can analyze the ways that traffic is controlled and coordinated. (A traffic light must be timed so that cars and pedestrians in *all four directions* can proceed safely; a traffic light obviates the need for a stop sign; a four-way stop sign is designated as such for drivers; electric WALK or DO NOT WALK signs must be coordinated with traffic lights, etc.)

4-12   **SS • LA**

Foundation for Architecture, Philadelphia

157. VOCABULARY: STREETSCAPES

aerial
alley
avenue

billboard
boulevard
back street
back yard
bench
bus stop

cross walk
curb
court, courtyard

dirt road
drain
driveway

electric wire
esplanade
expressway

facade elements
fence
freeway
fire hydrant

garden
gutter
gate
grate

highway

intersection

lawn
lane

meter
mailbox
mail storage box
mews
macadam
manhole cover
median

neon
newspaper stand

pedestrian
park
playground
piazza
plaza
public space
paving, pavement
pike
public
private

road
ramp
radio tower

safety
street
side street
subway station
stop sign
sign, signage
sidewalk
streetlight
"street furniture"
sewer

traffic, foot traffic
traffic light
traffic sign
telephone pole, telephone wire

vent

walkway
water silo

yard

K-12   **S • SS • LA**

Foundation for Architecture, Philadelphia

CITIES

Issues in community and city planning are presented as students begin cumulative and cooperative projects. Taking into account previous lessons, students plan and construct a model community, taking into account various aspects of public and private life.

CITIES

FOCUS ON PHILADELPHIA

158. WHAT IS A CITY?

The technical designation of the word "city" depends upon political organization rather than any concrete rule of size or population. For this reason, our use of the word is more generalized, and refers to a settled area of relatively dense population which has been organized around a variety of activities and interests. Have students brainstorm their associations with the word city, and help students see that the images that they have (tall buildings, traffic, etc.) are direct results of so many people living and working closely together.

K-12   **SS • LA**

Students can understand the distinctions between the words **rural**, **suburban**, and **urban** by brainstorming the different kinds of buildings and landscape features in each type of area:

* rural (country): farms, barns, single homes, pastures, fields, forests
* suburban (the **outskirts** of a city): housing developments, malls, low buildings, fewer trees and less open land than in the country
* urban (city): hi-rises and skyscrapers, few single homes, open land and trees limited to parks

4-12   **SS • LA**

Historically, cities developed in places where the **natural terrain** suited the needs of a large population. Rivers provided water and transportation, hills offered protection, etc. Aerial views and maps of a city in its natural context will give students a look at the natural boundaries that determined a city's placement and boundaries. Many cities have a distinct "old" section, often with historically designated buildings, that show early settlements right at the fork of two rivers or in the deepest part of a valley. Have students look at the names given to neighborhoods and streets for references that reflect the natural environment (Elm Street, Hidden Valley, Twin Forks, Hartford, etc.)

4-12   **S • SS • LA**

Have students extend their street addresses to include all of the progressions of community organizations, from the smallest unit (the individual) to the largest:

> name
> number and street
> neighborhood
> city (township, borough, etc.)
> county
> state
> country
> continent
> planet
> solar system

4-12   **S • SS • LA**

Have students develop **mental** and **cumulative** maps of their own cities. These maps will be more generalized than NEIGHBORHOOD maps, but should include certain features which the students will use when they are developing their own plans for cities.

- natural boundaries (rivers, mountains, valleys)
- major roadways
- building classifications (which sections are **residential**? **industrial**? **commercial**? etc.)

Students should come to understand that the city has been **organized** in an effort to meet a wide diversity of needs.

4-12   **M • SS • LA • A**

159. PLANNED OR UNPLANNED?

Point out to students that some cities were organized in advance, whereas other cities simply expanded as more people settled in them. It is often easy to see the difference in a map or aerial view. A city that follows a **plan** might be organized along clear geometric patterns with obvious focal points or a north-south axis. A city that developed through random settlement tends to sprawl in a more irregular pattern that might follow or reflect natural boundaries more directly. The Pyramid complexes, Babylon, and Rome are examples of ancient city planning, whereas Venice is a perfect example of a city that was developed around its natural setting. Examples of American city plans and planners include Philadelphia (Holmes), Savannah (Oglethorpe) and Washington, D.C. (L'Enfant).

Students should discuss the relative merits of each kind of city development. An unplanned city can develop "organically" according to the needs of its inhabitants, but if too many people try to settle in the same place, the result can be overcrowding or an imbalance of population, leading to health hazards and many other problems, as the natural resources may not be adequate. **City planners** try to think of ways to organize the people through the arrangement of the city, so that homes, roads, and factories are spread out in a way that will promote an efficient and healthy life for the inhabitants.

4-12   **SS • LA**

160. PLAN YOUR OWN CITY

Once students have become aware of the importance of city planning, they will be ready to begin developing their own plan as a cooperative project. Have students brainstorm as many different kinds of buildings as possible. Write list on board or large paper; provoke with questions (What if you want to go out to eat? What if your car needs oil?)

From this list, students will now establish priorities for which buildings should be included in their model city. The class is now acting as a community and must make decisions as a group. Students should be encouraged to make suggestions and offer valid reasons for their choices; this and other planning discussions will provoke **debate**, **negotiation**, and **arbitration**; the class must develop a system to establish final decisions. Point out that **citizens** actually do have the power to organize town meetings and exert their influence on city growth.

K-12   **SS • LA**

161. DESIGN A BUILDING FOR YOUR CITY

Once the students have made a group decision about what types of buildings to include in their city, each student will choose one to design and construct in model form. As in Activity #136, each student-architect must develop this design through a series of stages:

- make a **journal** of ideas in words and drawings
- establish the building's **function**
- establish the building's **size**
- establish **who will use** the building, including an estimate of the largest group of people to be accomodated at one time
- establish the **materials** to be used
- make a **floor plan** (or plans)
- draw the front **elevation** (facade)
- construct a **model**

Be sure that students maintain the same **scale** by using a pipe-cleaner figure or equivalent.

K-12   **S • M • SS • LA • A**

Foundation for Architecture, Philadelphia

162. ZONING

Following are several ways to layout a model community. Regardless of which arrangement is used, the students must decide as a group how their buildings are to be arranged. Explain that **zoning** laws exist to control the placement of different kinds of businesses and structures to protect communities. Students can look for **zoning notices** posted on buildings, which are a public declaration of an owner's intended use for a building. The notice is posted so that the neighbors have a chance to review the plan at a zoning commission meeting. Students can discuss why certain businesses might be undesirable. (For example, too many bars often create noisy crowds late at night; a movie theatre could use up all the residents' parking spaces, a tall building might block the sunlight from a park, etc.)

Students should refer to the classifications of buildings and make clear decisions about the relationship of residential, commercial, industrial, recreational, institutional, and monumental buildings in their community. Which types should be separate? Which types can be mixed together? (For example, residential buildings are preferred away from industrial; monuments are often found in isolation or in parklands; commercial and institutional buildings are easily mixed, etc.)

4-12   **SS • LA**

163. ESTABLISH A ZONING COMMISSION

Students can elect a **zoning commission** to consider possible controversies about where students want to put their buildings. The commissioners will listen to the arguments and then, through **arbitration**, will make a final decision. The commissioners are free to suggest compromises. (For example, if the "neighbors" are concerned that a large apartment building will use up all local parking, the commission can suggest that the architect include an underground parking lot. If two students want to build hotels on the same lot on the waterfront, the commission can suggest that one hotel could be made low so that the hotel behind it could be higher and both would have full view of the water.)

6-12   **SS • LA**

164. MODEL CITY LAYOUTS

There are many ways for your students to lay out their model communities. The following list presents some suggestions to be adapted according to time and curricular focus.

A. CITY INTERSECTION

On large paper, draw the intersection of two streets that includes sites for four parks at the corners.

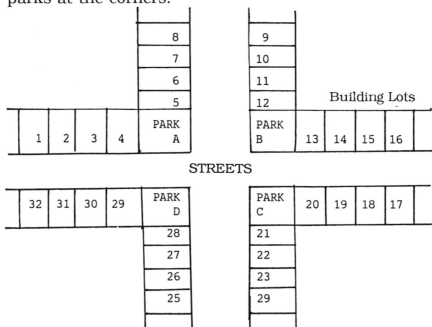

The students will divide themselves into four groups (A, B, C, D) by drawing lot numbers. In groups, they will make planning decisions for their sections based on community needs, building types, and park use. Each group will have to interact with the others to develop a reasonable overall plan.

(This base is an excellent site for ROWHOUSE models; be sure to reconcile the scale of the base to the scale of the models.)

Students may add additional buildings, street furniture, traffic systems, and landscaping.

K-12   **M • SS • LA • A**

B. STREET GRID

On very large paper, students will develop a geometric street **grid**; main streets run **parallel** to each other with cross-streets running **perpendicular** to the main streets (as in the layout of Manhattan Island). Students might want to introduce one **diagonal** street, a central **park**, or a couple of **circles** into the grid, but these features should not interfere with the regularity of the rest of the grid and should be used for a particular purpose. Students should consider these aspects:

- orientation of streets in relation to the cardinal points (North, East, South, West)
- central street axis, perhaps broader than the other streets
- main and secondary streets of different widths for different uses (commercial vs. residential)
- placement of commercial, industrial, recreational, and residential buildings or clusters
- street names

Once the grid has been laid out, students will choose various buildings to design and construct.

K-12   M • SS • LA • A

C. CONTOUR AND TOPOGRAPHIC MAPS

Introduce students to a **contour** map, showing "layers" of progressive elevation through **concentric** contours. Label hill, valley, mountain, plateau, river basin, etc. Have students cut the various layers out of corrugated cardboard and glue them together to bring the two-dimensional map into the third dimension; this product is a **topographic** map (see illustration).

A contour map shows variations of elevation through **concentric contours**.

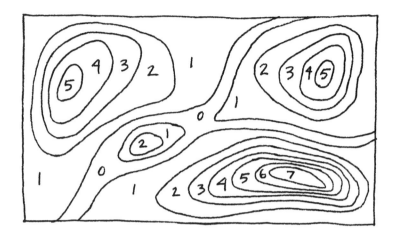

CONTOUR MAP

For scale, each number might represent 10 feet, so that this map shows two hills which are 50 feet high, an island 20 feet high, and a mountain 70 feet high. (The river is at 0 feet, or sea level).

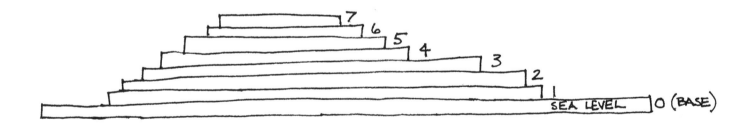

TOPOGRAPHIC MODEL

Students can add as many layers as they wish provided that each layer is smaller than the one below it and reflects the contours of the preceeding layer.

4-12   **S • M • SS • LA • A**

Foundation for Architecture, Philadelphia

Once students have a topographic base, they should discuss the various ways a city might be planned in very uneven terrain.

- residential: Should homes be up high for the view or nestled in a valley, protected from the wind?
- commercial: Should commercial buildings be spread out for the convenience of shoppers or clustered together, as in a business district or mall?
- industrial: How close should industrial buildings be to homes? Should the industrial section have access to a river (for energy and transportation)? How will the river be protected from industrial pollution?
- monumental: What sites would be effective for monuments?
- recreational: What would be good locations for a ski lift or an ice skating rink? Where should a movie house be put?
- roadways and bridges: How will the various sections of the city be connected?

Students must decide whether they want to impose a geometric plan on the terrain or follow the natural contours. Once these decisions are made, students will plan and construct the structures needed for their model city.

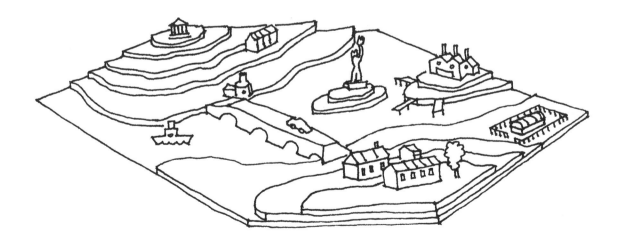

Foundation for Architecture, Philadelphia

D. LANDSCAPE

On a large piece of heavy cardboard or plywood, plan a landscape with students to be developed in papier mache or plaster gauze. The students should consider not only the **topography** but also the **climate** of this landscape, with the understanding that they are establishing the environment for their model city and that this environment will have an impact on their design criteria. (Students can form groups and develop different climates and terrains for different kinds of cities.)

Students should be able to name the geographic features of the landscape model and explain how their city plans "fit" the landscape and the climate implied by it. Each student will design and construct a building and decide on an appropriate location.

4-12   **S • SS • LA • A**

E. FOUND OBJECTS

Students with less developed motor skills can collect found objects and scraps to use for a model city. Hair curlers, corks, blocks, small boxes (match boxes, individual cereal boxes, etc.), plastic or styrofoam caps, clothespins, egg-carton sections, and many other objects can be assembled to represent a model city. Students should make clear decisions about what kinds of structures the objects represent and arrange them according to an overall plan. By leaving the objects unpainted, their patterns and words will resemble the patterns and signage of a real city.

K-12   **SS • LA • A**

FOCUS ON PHILADELPHIA

Educators in the Delaware Valley have a great resource in Philadelphia, a city which was carefully planned by William Penn and Thomas Holme in 1682 and is today a virtual "museum of architecture." Much of its original form and structures remain intact, and succeeding generations of technological development and stylistic changes are clearly evident. Many of Philadelphia's architects and much of its architecture are known internationally. The Philadelphia Foundation for Architecture can help develop tours or provide further information for a class trip.

● ● ●

The following activities are appropriate for students who live in or around Philadelphia, although they can be adapted to other cities.

165. HOW MUCH DO YOU KNOW ABOUT PHILADELPHIA?

Begin your study of Philadelphia by finding out what information your students already have. As a diagnostic exercise, this will help you gauge the level of the students' sophistication and will give you insight into their perspectives. Students in the outer reaches of the city limits may be surprisingly unfamiliar with Center City.

Have students brainstorm the following issues as a group or in individual notes to be shared with the class:

- What is the climate of Philadelphia?
- Can you name any of the natural boundaries or features of Philadelphia? (rivers, valleys, etc.)
- Name as many of the following as you can:
  - neighborhoods
  - buildings
  - parks
  - bridges
  - roads
- What adjectives would you use to describe Philadelphia?
- What does the word *Philadelphia* mean? Who founded the city? What does the word *Pennsylvania* mean?
- What are some other things you can think of that make Philadelphia special?

K-12   **SS • LA**

Students should make **mental maps** of Philadelphia which will show their subjective perceptions of the city. Students should then begin to develop **cumulative maps** based on their increasing knowledge.

4-12   **SS • LA • A**

---

166. PENN'S PLAN FOR PHILADELPHIA

Show a slide (or prepare a large scale version) of **William Penn**'s original layout for the streets of Philadelphia. Let the students study the map and try to find as many things possible that they recognize. Stress that this early design has been extremely effective, as most of it is still intact. Here is a brief history of the plan (the map drawn by **Thomas Holme** follows):

Cities planned prior to their development are comparatively rare. In the settlement of America, none was as carefully planned as Philadelphia.

The basic plan for the city was conceived by William Penn in 1682 and was laid out by Thomas Holme, his surveyor-general. The plan structured an area of about 1280 acres, 2 miles long and one mile wide, with a grid system of roads and five major squares. Two major roads bisected the city from north to south and from east to west, called Broad Street and High Street (later renamed Market Street). These streets were 100 feet wide and the rest of the streets were 50 feet wide. The north and south streets were numbered consecutively from both rivers, although now, the streets are numbered consecutively west from the Delaware River. The east-west streets are named after principal trees in the region.

At the intersection of the two major street axes, Penn placed a square to be used for a "public building", where City Hall stands today. Each of the quadrants defined by these axes has its own major square set aside for common use and enjoyment by all citizens.

This plan survived well for 200 years. This one major change was the diagonal of the Benjamin Franklin Parkway cutting across the grid. The original concept introduced in 1892, was intended to create a diagonal vista that would break the monotony of the grid.

Philadelphia City Planning Commission 1976

4-12   **M • SS**

167. THE PENN/HOLME PLAN FOR PHILADELPHIA: 1682

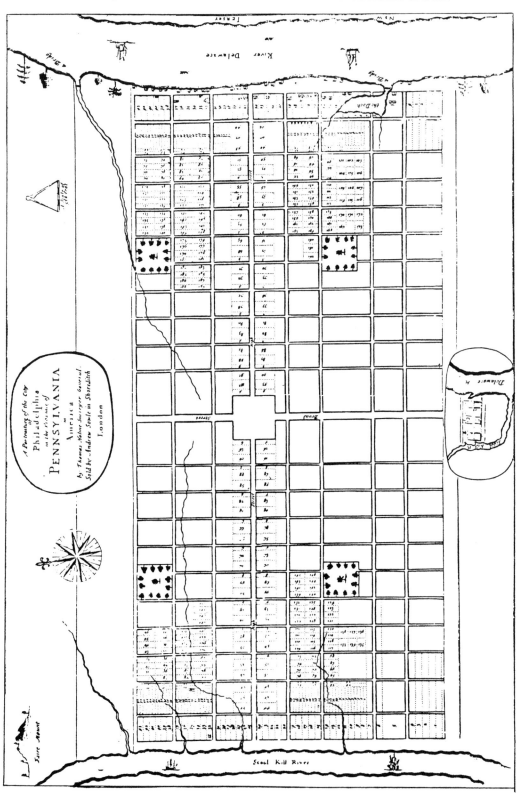

Foundation for Architecture, Philadelphia

168. CENTER CITY: OLD AND NEW

Prepare maps of:

- the Penn/Holme Plan
- a map of contemporary Center City (following)
- a map of Philadelphia showing neighborhoods (following)

Students will use the first two maps to find aspects of the original **plan** that are still intact and to notice essential changes; the third map will show the boundaries of Center City in context and the directions in which the city has grown. (Note that this section of the city is located at the narrowest point between the Schuylkill and Delaware Rivers.)

4-12   **M • SS**

Students can "role-play" the original structure of Center City. The "parts" include:

- the Delaware River
- the Schuylkill River
- Broad Street (N - S)
- High Street (now Market Street) (E - W)
- the five squares:
  - Center Square
  - Washington Square (SE)
  - Rittenhouse Square (SW)
  - Logan Square (NW)
  - Franklin Square (NE)
- Vine Street
- South Street

Holding cards labelled with the various parts, students will position themselves in the classroom to correspond to the map. Students who portray rivers and streets can lie down and stretch out in the correct direction; students who portray the five squares can stoop down.

K-6   **SS**

Foundation for Architecture, Philadelphia

From the map of present-day Center City, students should note the similarities and differences between the two. All of the above-mentioned features still exist, although High Street is now Market Street and Logan Square has become a Circle. The obvious addition is the diagonal of the Benjamin Franklin Parkway (1892) which now links City Hall, Logan Circle and the Philadelphia Museum of Art. (A class that is "role-playing" the city can add these features, with the student in the central square now standing with arms arched overhead to indicate the tower of City Hall.)

Another aspect of the original plan that has survived is the designation of N-S streets (parallel to Broad Street) by **numbers** and of E-W streets (parallel to Market Street) by the names of **trees** indigenous to the Delaware Valley (Walnut, Chestnut, Spruce, Pine, etc.). Discuss with students the advantage of naming the streets in this way.

Invite students to name and locate other landmarks of contemporary Philadelphia, either on the map or in role-play; Main Post Office, 30th Street Station, the Ben Franklin Bridge, the Walt Whitman Bridge (South of the map), the Rodin Museum, the Free Library, Penn's Landing, etc.

K-12   M • SS

Use the map of Philadelphia's Neighborhoods to show students how Center City fits into the context of the present city limits, and have students find their own neighborhoods.

K-12   M • SS

169. PRESENT-DAY CENTER CITY

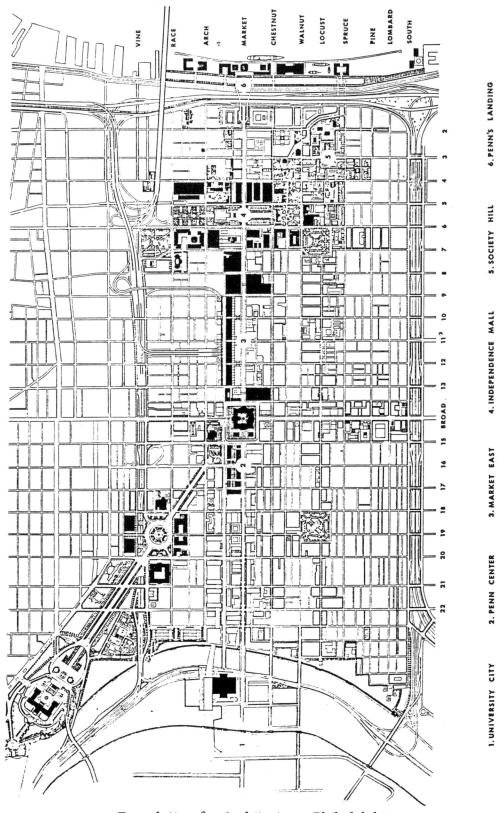

Foundation for Architecture, Philadelphia

170. PHILADELPHIA'S NEIGHBORHOODS

CENTER CITY (1–6)

1. Logan Circle
2. Chinatown
3. Old City
4. Society Hill
5. Washington Square
6. Rittenhouse

7. Schuylkill
8. Southwest Center City
9. Hawthorne
10. Bell Vista
11. Queen Village
12. Pennsport
13. Wharton
14. Point Breeze
15. Grays Ferry
16. Girard Estate
17. Packer Park
18. Whitman
19. Eastwick
20. Elmwood
21. Paschall
22. Kingsessing
23. Southwest Schuylkill
24. Cobbs Creek
25. Garden Court
26. Cedar Park
27. Spruce Hill
28. University City
29. Powelton
30. Mantua
31. Belmont
32. Mill Creek
33. Haddington
34. Overbrook
35. Carroll Park
36. Parkside

37. Wynnefield
38. Wynnefield Heights
39. Spring Garden
40. Poplar
41. Northern Liberties
42. Francisville
43. Fairmount
44. Olde Kensington
45. Ludlow
46. Yorktown
47. North Central
48. Sharswood
49. Brewerytown
50. Strawberry Mansion
51. Stanton
52. Hartranft
53. Franklinville
54. Nicetown-Tioga
55. Allegheny West
56. Hunting Park
57. Fishtown
58. Kensington
59. West Kensington
60. Feltonville
61. Juniata
62. Richmond
63. Bridesburg
64. Andorra
65. Upper Roxborough
66. Roxborough
67. Manayunk
68. East Falls
69. Germantown
70. Wister
71. Morton
72. East Mt. Airy
73. West Mt. Airy
74. Chestnut Hill
75. Cedarbrook
76. West Oak Lane
77. Logan
78. East Oak Lane
79. Olney
80. Lawncrest
81. Summerdale
82. Northwood
83. Frankford
84. Wissinoming
85. Tacony
86. Mayfair
87. Oxford Circle
88. Burholme
89. Fox Chase
90. Rhawnhurst
91. Lexington Park
92. Holmesburg
93. Upper Holmesburg
94. Torresdale
95. Academy Gardens
96. Ashton-Woodenbridge
97. Pennypack Woods
98. Winchester Park
99. Pennypack
100. Bustleton
101. West Torresdale
102. Morrell Park
103. Crestmont Farms
104. Millbrook
105. Modena Park
106. Parkwood Manor
107. Mechanicsville
108. Byberry
109. Somerton

Foundation for Architecture, Philadelphia

171. ROWHOUSES

Hand out to students a brief history of the Philadelphia rowhouse (following).

Discuss the reasons for having houses in a row (shared walls mean more houses for less money in less space).

Have each student draw a single facade on a paper cut to fit the bottom of a shoebox. Color and decorate; glue onto the shoeboxes; arrange into a continuous facade. Determine scale by establishing the same door size on each facade.

4-12   **SS • LA • A**

Hand out to students the simple image of a repetitive rowhouse facade (page 184). Using their facade vocabularies, have the students try to make each unit as different as possible from the others, using color, pattern (stone, brick, stucco, siding), architectural elements and whimsy.

Help students find ideas through slides of rowhouses or by taking a walk through a rowhouse neighborhood. Take photographs or make sketches. Take a driving tour through areas of Philadelphia to see why Philadelphia is famous for its rowhouses.

K-12   **SS • LA • A**

Use the following rowhouse kit for students to make models of rowhouses. Encourage students to be imaginative in their facades to avoid monotonous repetition.

6-12   **M • SS • A**

172. HISTORY OF THE ROWHOUSE

MODEL PHILADELPHIA HOUSE.
Exhibited at the World's Columbian
Exposition, 1893.
SPECULATION HOUSE

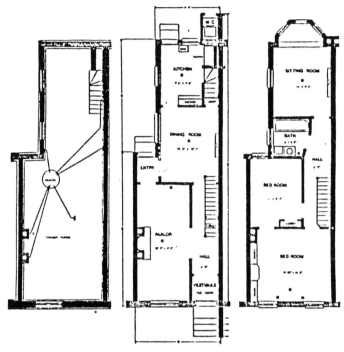

FLOOR PLANS—MODEL PHILADELPHIA HOUSE
World's Columbian Exposition, 1893.

SPECULATION HOUSE

This version of the Philadelphia row house was exhibited at the World's Columbian Exhibition at St. Louis in 1893. It was considered an excellent example of housing which was available to ordinary citizens, but which contained amenities such as good light and air, private open space, and the financial benefits of individual ownership. Note especially in this example the separate entrance to the garden from the parlor, the reduction of the hallway and circulation space to a minimum, central heating and the impressive amount of decoration on the facade.

Philadelphia Planning Commission, 1976

4-12   **SS • LA**

Foundation for Architecture, Philadelphia

173. ROWHOUSE FACADES

How different can you make these facades look?

K-12   **SS • A**

Foundation for Architecture, Philadelphia

174. ROWHOUSE KIT

Introduce students to the history and aspects of rowhouses. Point out their great prevalence in Philadelphia through a walk or a driving tour.

Students should spend some time making large scale rowhouse facades before proceeding to the rowhouse kit. The kit shows a pattern for pieces that are glued together to form a model that is:

- 6" wide
- 9" high
- 12" deep
- has two floors and a roof
- has one exposed rear wall so that the interior floors will show

(Wall B is optional except for the house at the end of the row, as the houses will all share one wall when the houses are put together.) Facades should be decorated before assembly.

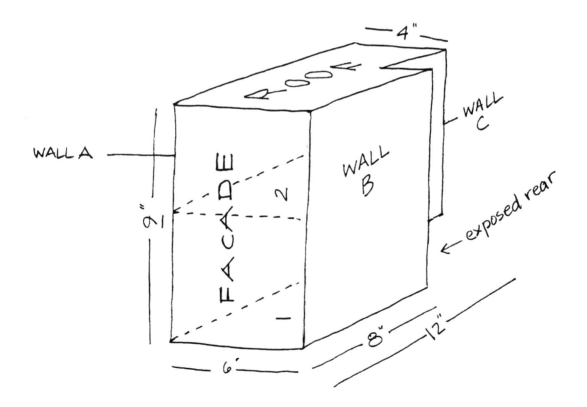

Foundation for Architecture, Philadelphia

ROWHOUSE KIT

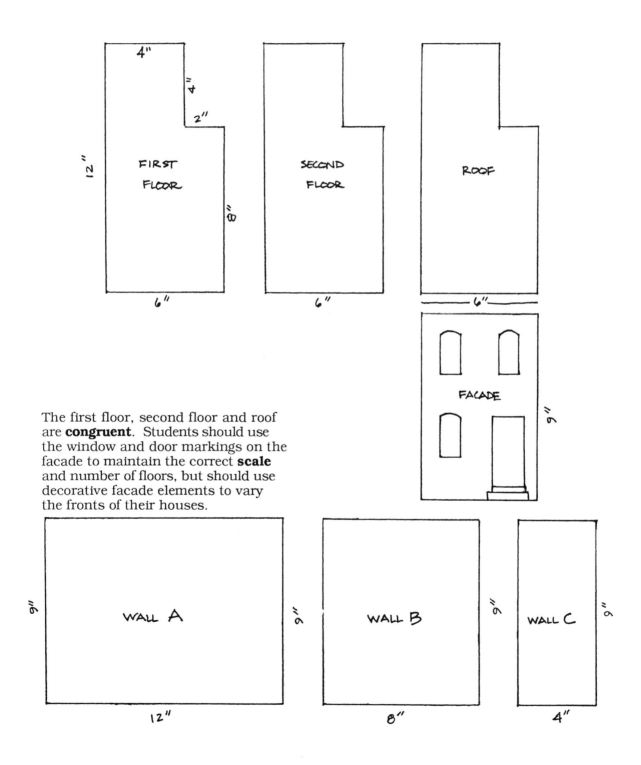

The first floor, second floor and roof are **congruent**. Students should use the window and door markings on the facade to maintain the correct **scale** and number of floors, but should use decorative facade elements to vary the fronts of their houses.

Foundation for Architecture, Philadelphia

BIBLIOGRAPHY

Topics in built environment education are so extensive
that this publication can only hope to suggest the many
possible directions. This Bibliography lists some of the
many first-rate books developed for the classroom
according to specific topics. Some may be currently out of
print, but all are available at the Resource Center of the
Foundation for Architecture, Philadelphia.

BIBLIOGRAPHY

Perception

(8-12)   ***Experiencing Architecture.*** Steen Rassmussen. MIT Press: Cambridge, MA, 1959.

(4-12)   ***Looking and Seeing.*** Kurt Rowland. Ginn: London, 1964.
        Book 1: Pattern and Shape
        Book 2: The Development of Shape
        Book 3: The Shapes We Need
        Book 4: The Shape of Towns

(4-8)   ***Streets.*** Serge Cvijanovic and Galila Spero. Harwell Associates: Convent Station, NJ, 1976.

History

(6-12)   ***Architecture Without Architects.*** Bernard Rudofsky. Doubleday and Company, Inc.: Garden City, NY, 1964.

(4-12)   ***The Buildings of Ancient Greece.*** Helen and Richard Leacroft. Addison-Wesley: Reading, MA, 1969.

(K-12)   ***Castle.*** David Macaulay. Houghton Mifflin Company: Boston, 1977.

(K-12)   ***Cathedral.*** David Macaulay. Houghton Mifflin Company: Boston, 1973.

(4-12)   ***Grand Constructions.*** Gian Paolo Ceserani and Piero Ventura. G.P. Putnam's Sons: NY, 1983.

(K-12)   ***Pyramid.*** David Macaulay. Houghton Mifflin Company: Boston: 1975.

(4-12)   ***The Seven Wonders of the World.*** Kenneth McLeish. Cambridge University Press: NY, 1985.

Foundation for Architecture, Philadelphia

Structures

(K-6) *Animals Build Amazing Homes.* Hedda Nussbaum. Random House: NY, 1979.

(4-12) *Bridges: A Project Book.* Anne and Scott MacGregor. Lothrop, Lee and Shepard Books: NY, 1980.

(4-12) *Domes: A Project Book.* Anne and Scott MacGregor. Lothrop, Lee and Shepard Books: NY, 1981.

(4-8) *Housebuilding for Children.* Les Walker. Overlook Press: Woodstock, NY, 1977

(K-12) *Underground.* David Macaulay. Houghton Mifflin Company: Boston, 1976.

(4-12) *Skyscrapers: A Project Book.* Anne and Scott MacGregor. Lothrop, Lee and Shepard Books: NY 1980.

Cities

(4-12) *Cities: Comparison of Form and Scale.* Richard Saul Wurman. Joshua Press: Philadelphia, 1974.

(8-12) *Design of Cities.* Edmund Bacon. Penguin Books: NY, 1976.

(8-12) *The Language of Cities.* Fran P. Hosken. Schenkman Publishing Company, Inc.: Cambridge, MA, 1972.

(8-12) *Urban Open Spaces.* Lisa Taylor, Editor. Rizzoli: NY 1981.

Architecture of the United States

(6-12) *American Shelter: An Illustrated Encyclopedia of the American Home.* Lester Walker. Overlook Press: Woodstock, NY 1981.

(6-12) *Identifying American Architecture: A Pictorial Guide to Styles and Terms, 1600-1945.* John J.G. Blumenson. American Association for State and Local History: Nashville, TN, 1977.

Architecture of Philadelphia

(6-12)   *Philadelphia Architecture: A Guide to the City.* Prepared for the Foundation for Architecture, Philadelphia, by the Group for Environmental Education, Inc.; John Andrew Gallery, General Editor. MIT Press: Cambridge, MA 1984.

(K-12)   *Still Philadelphia: A Photographic Essay.* Frederic M. Miller, Morris J. Vogel and Allen F. Davis. Temple University Press: Philadelphia, 1983.

(8-12)   *Walking Tours of Historic Philadelphia.* John Francis Marion. ISHI Publications: Philadelphia, 1974.

Activity Books

(4-12)   *Architecture: A Book of Projects for Young People.* Forrest Wilson. Reinhold Book Corporation: NY, 1968.

(4-12)   *Architecture is Elementary: Visual Thinking Through Architectural Concepts.* Nathan B. Winters. Peregrine Smith Books: Salt Lake City, 1986.

(K-12)   *Beginning Experiences in Architecture: A Guide for the Elementary School Teacher.* George E. Trogler. Van Nostrand Reinhold Company: NY, 1972.

(4-12)   *Blueprints: A Built Environment Education Program.* Marjorie Wintermute. Washington County Education Service District: Portland, OR, 1983.

(4-12)   *Environmental Encounter: Experiences in Decision-Making for the Built and Natural Environment.* Joanne Henderson Pratt, James Pratt, Sarah Barnett Moore and William T. Moore, M.D. Reverchon Press: Dallas, TX, 1979.

(4-12)   *Historic Preservation Education.* Carol D. Holden, Gary L. Olsen and Michele R. Olsen. Historic Preservation Education Project: Champaign, IL, 1980.

(6-12)   ***Our Man Made Environment: Book 7.*** Alan Levy, William B. Chapman, Richard Saul Wurman. Group for Environmental Education (GEE!): Philadelphia, 1970.

(4-12)   ***People in Places: Experiencing, Using and Changing the Built Environment.*** Jay Farbstein and Min Kantrowitz. Prentice-Hall Inc.: Englewood Cliffs, NJ, 1978.

(4-8)   ***Streetscape: Activity Guide.*** Joyce Meschan, Editor. Vision, The Center for Environmental Design and Education: Cambridge, MA, 1980.

(4-12)   ***Students, Structures, Spaces: Activities in the Built Environment.*** Aase Eriksen and Marjorie Wintermute. Addison-Wesley: Reading, MA, 1983.

Math Activities

(K-8)   ***MARA (Mathematics/Architecture Related Activities).*** The University of the State of New York, State Education Department: Albany, NY, 1982.

Science Activities

(8-12)   ***Architecture and Engineering: An Illustrated Teacher's Manual of Why Buildings Stand Up.*** Mario Salvadori and Michael Tempel. New York Academy of Sciences: NY, 1983.

(6-12)   ***Architecture and Interior Environment: A Book of Projects for Young Adults.*** Forrest Wilson. Van Nostrand Reinhold Company: NY, 1972.

Reference

(8-12) *The Architecture Book.* Norval White. Knopf: NY, 1976.

(8-12) *Architectural Styles.* Herbert Pothorn. Facts on File Publications: NY, 1979.

(K-12) *Great Architecture of the World.* John Julius Norwich, General Editor. Bonanza Books: NY, 1982.

(K-12) *Notebooks from the Architecture in Education Program* Architecture students from the University of Pennsylvania and Temple University, as part of their credit for participation in the AIE Program, are required to prepare a Notebook on the lessons developed by their teaching teams. These Notebooks are available (for reference use only) at the Resource Center of the Foundation for Architecture, Philadelphia.

NOTES

NOTES

NOTES